ACTIVE
INVE$TING

REVISED EDITION

HOW TO **MANAGE** YOUR PORTFOLIO LIKE A PROFESSIONAL IN **LESS THAN ONE** HOUR A WEEK

ALAN HULL

Wrightbooks

First published 2009 by Wrightbooks
an imprint of John Wiley & Sons Australia, Ltd
42 McDougall Street, Milton Qld 4064

Office also in Melbourne

Typeset in Berkeley LT 11pt/14pt

© Alan Hull 2009

The moral rights of the author have been asserted

Reprinted in 2010 and 2011

National Library of Australia Cataloguing-in-Publication data:

Author:	Hull, Alan, 1962-
Title:	Active investing: how to manage your portfolio like a professional in less than one hour a week / Alan Hull.
Edition:	Rev ed.
ISBN:	9781742168630 (pbk.)
Notes:	Includes index.
Subjects:	Investments — Handbooks, manuals, etc. Stock exchanges.
Dewey Number:	332.678

Cover design by Brad Maxwell

Cover image of clock © Shutterstock/ iDesign

Microsoft Excel screen shots reprinted with permission from Microsoft Corporation.

Charts on pages 166, 167 and 174 by MetaStock.

All other charts created by TradeStation. © TradeStation Technologies, Inc. All rights reserved.

Printed in China by Printplus Limited

10 9 8 7 6 5

Disclaimer
The material in this publication is of the nature of general comment only, and does not represent professional advice. It is not intended to provide specific guidance for particular circumstances and it should not be relied on as the basis for any decision to take action or not take action on any matter which it covers. Readers should obtain professional advice where appropriate, before making any such decision. To the maximum extent permitted by law, the author and publisher disclaim all responsibility and liability to any person, arising directly or indirectly from any person taking or not taking action based upon the information in this publication.

Contents

In memory of
Shani Hull and Leigh Burkitt
Life is a fragile thing that should never be taken for granted

Acknowledgements

Simon Sherwood, finance author and all-round nice guy
This revised edition is only possible because of your help and encouragement.

Matt Livingston, personal assistant and sounding-board
I have never met anyone with your ability to spend so much time with me and not go mad (or at least get very frustrated).

Jeffrey Shaw, stockbroker
A man who makes his living by putting his clients first.

Braden Gardiner, stockbroker
Another adviser who doesn't put his own interests before those of his clients.

Debra Hull, my wife and best friend
Without you in my life I would achieve little.

Kathryn and Matthew Hull, my little mates
Watching you grow up keeps me from growing old.

About the author

A second generation share trader, Alan Hull owned his first share at the age of eight. As a result of this early introduction to the stock market, most of the lessons the average investor learns in their adult life were second nature to Alan by the time he was 21.

With a keen interest in mathematics, Alan was an IT expert from the early days of personal computing. Employing this combination of skills, as well as market experience over the past two decades, Alan is now one of Australia's leading stock market professionals. He is highly respected within the Australian investment industry, regularly writing articles and presenting for the Australian Securities Exchange, the Australian Technical Analysts Association, the Australian Investors Association, and the Traders and Investors Expo. Furthermore, in addition to writing his own best-selling books, he has contributed to other publications such as the best-selling *Top Stocks* series by Martin Roth, and Daryl Guppy's *Better Stock Trading*.

Not content with being a private trader, author and educator, Alan is also a licensed financial adviser with his own managed fund. Over the past few years, he has successfully managed millions of dollars of other people's money, consistently beating all the major ASX market averages. One of Alan's most notable decisions as a funds manager was to move his entire fund to cash at the start of August 2007, preserving his client's capital throughout one of the worst global financial crises of the past century.

With a focus on the practical, Alan has distilled much of his market wisdom into this revised edition of his best-seller, *Active Investing*.

Preface

I owned my first share at the age of eight. It was a birthday present from my father and it cost $5. I can't recall the name of it, but I remember that I chose it and it doubled in price during the next six months. As my birthday is in June, it was a good Christmas that year! In 1970, $10 was a lot of money to an eight year old. I spent my fortune on lollies for myself and presents for my siblings.

When I turned nine, my father gave me another $5 to buy a share, but this time he advised me on what to buy. The share price fell steadily in the following months and eventually I went to my father for more advice. I have never forgotten his words: 'If the share price is going up you'll make money, but if it's going down you'll lose money'. With the reflex thinking of a nine year old, I asked him to sell the share. I then asked him if he was going to give me back my original $5. He took a deep breath, looked at me and paused—a sure sign of bad news. He gently told me that I could only get back the current value of the share, and that if I didn't want to rely on advice from others then I should learn about shares for myself. As history shows, I took his advice.

When I look around me today it is of little surprise that the average 'mum and dad' investor is often paralysed by confusion. There are too many choices, too many opinions, too many financial products and numerous specific and non-specific books on investment.

Active Investing is my response to this confusion. Average investors want to profit from stock market investments by making their own decisions, without risking the family home or their hard-earned savings. They want to be hands-on when it comes to managing their share portfolios. They want to be *active investors*.

Active investing, as I present it in this book, is simple. It takes less than one hour a week to implement and combines many different types of investment techniques into one fluid approach. There is a degree of validity to every method currently employed by investors and traders, and active investing acknowledges this by taking everything into consideration. However, one of the key elements to success in the marketplace is to understand that survival depends on market experience and not on being in charge of all the facts. The following story illustrates this point.

It's a jungle out there

It's a blustery day and I'm chairing a meeting of the 'Sunday Traders Club'. We meet on the first Sunday of every month for several hours to swap opinions and information and to analyse a few stocks. I'm sitting at a table facing an audience of 50 or so, among whom are long-term investors, newcomers to the stock market and an assortment of traders. Many hold investments in the property market as well as in the sharemarket. The members of the group come from a range of occupations; there are truck drivers, home-based business operators, doctors and retirees. Our ages vary from mid 30s to mid 70s.

It's discussion time and Douglas, a relative newcomer, has stood up and asked the room about a stock he holds—he can't decide what to do with it. We all know his line of questioning as this is the third month in a row that he has interrogated us for our collective opinion. Signs of disinterest are evident around the room.

He receives the same responses as he has on the last two occasions. The investors suggest reviewing the company's fundamentals and future prospects to ascertain whether holding over the longer term would be prudent, while the traders and chartists offer analysis and technical strategies for assessing share price movements.

Harold, a regular attendee who is not known for his tolerance, has had enough. He begins reciting a summary of the day's opinions for Douglas. At the end of the summary, he asks Douglas if he is happy with the group's responses. With a smile Douglas answers, 'Yes, thanks everyone', and starts to sit down. Harold loudly asks Douglas to stay standing, with an urgency that brings Douglas swiftly back to a standing position and has him glaring at Harold with an expression that is both angry and apprehensive.

In a businesslike tone Harold reminds him that he has rained questions on the group for the past three months and, by his own admission, is now in possession of all the relevant facts. Continuing in a calm voice, Harold then suggests that it would now be reasonable for Douglas to make a command decision about what he's going to do with this particular stock. Before Douglas can offer his usual deflection of 'I'm going to think about it for a while', Harold chimes in first with: 'Three months, Douglas. What's your decision?'

You must take action

Douglas's inertia reminds me of a young deer, straying from the jungle on to bitumen for the first time, at dusk. In the distance several spots of light can be seen and appear to be growing larger. As they are still far away and present no immediate danger, the young animal stays where it is and holds them in its gaze.

The driver of the fast-approaching semi-trailer stares through the windshield at the deer caught in his headlights, willing it to move out of his way. He releases his frustration in the confines of the vehicle's cabin, yelling, 'Left or right you dumb animal, just move!' Oblivious of the expletives the deer freezes, suddenly terrified by the audible protests of the downshifting transmission. As the truck slows, the driver begins dipping his headlights and using the air horn, but he's not prepared to stop or swerve for the benefit of a single, dumb animal. Besides, all it has to do is move — which way doesn't matter.

The marketplace is like the huge semi-trailer. It is a powerful machine comprising thousands of moving parts, large and small — the small speculators, the investors trying to build wealth over time, the company directors, the stockbrokers and many, many more on the periphery. If we, the user, want more information, faster delivery of information, different information, or the ability to buy and sell shares from overseas, then the machine will adapt to these demands. It's there to serve us and its evolution is driven by our needs.

The evolutionary process has accelerated, with the help of technology, to the point where the machine is even beginning to adapt to needs that it anticipates we will have in the future.

Like the semi-trailer hurtling towards the deer, the marketplace won't stop to avoid injury to the unsuspecting. It may provide education, offer expert advice, facilitate fast and easy access to information and do anything else that users may want of it, but it won't stop, backup and refund your money.

Investors like Douglas—the 'mum and dad' investors—trying to graduate to the next level may be armed with knowledge after having read books on fundamental analysis (including the compulsory text on Warren Buffett); they may even have bought a computer and sophisticated (read 'expensive') investment software to boot. But this is all useless if they are paralysed like the deer and unable to take action.

Douglas's list of questions just seems to grow at every meeting, parallel with the growth in his knowledge. He's on the information merry-go-round, looking for the magic bullet that will break the cycle. He's even attended some of the 'get rich quick' courses that cost the equivalent of an overseas family holiday. Then, having become disillusioned with that avenue of endeavour, he's turned to the 'how to manage your poverty' courses that don't hit the hip pocket quite so hard. But none of them have provided the solutions he went hunting for in the first place.

It all seemed so straightforward when he and his wife had that initial discussion about using a sensible, balanced and informed approach to actively improving their financial future. He is fully committed to this pursuit and has invested large amounts of time and money in his education, to the point where I believe he knows more than I do. Yet, like the deer in the headlights, he is standing at the meeting, staring at me with his eyes pleading—unable to make a decision.

Predator or prey?

Douglas must face the fact that the stock market will not pause while he considers his investment decisions. Worse, the longer he hesitates, the fewer his options will become. While he doesn't take any action there are plenty of market participants who will.

A deer is never the predator, always the prey, and Mother Nature has equipped it for this role; all the deer's senses are designed to home in on danger and trigger it to flight. Its long skinny legs are capable of propelling it at high speed over a variety of terrain, including tall native grass. This speed, coupled with the ability to switch direction as if bouncing off an invisible wall, makes the deer an elusive meal for any adversary, provided it can take action.

A couple of the full-time traders at the back of the room shoot quick, knowing glances at each other. They begin to move in their seats, unable to keep still. These guys talk to each other during the coffee break but always sit apart during meetings, as if sitting together were breaking some kind of rule. Few in the audience know they're full-time traders, and they seem to prefer it that way. I quickly scan the sea of faces to observe the response to this still brief but pregnant silence. One of the traders shoots me a grin. It's only this small band of traders that *aren't* staring at me with a puzzled expression, or at Douglas with 'we're waiting' written all over their faces.

While a lot of professional traders work alone, there are many who network with others to share their talents in order to exploit opportunities that would be lost to them as individuals. This particular small band of experienced traders, are part of a nationwide group of similar self-styled market professionals. Their individual knowledge and skills cover a wide spectrum, and by networking, all have access to a formidable arsenal of market information and trading tactics. This arsenal can be drawn upon at a moment's notice and instantly distributed to the entire network, thanks to email and online discussion forums. Like a pack of hyenas, they know that their individual survival depends on their success as a group and they would not hesitate to profit from the indecision of others. Indecisive people are prone to rumours and their own emotions causing them to either hesitate or overreact. These traders all know the lesson of indecision and their bank accounts and trading ledgers bear the scars.

Others in the room might think that the magic bullet is to gain admission to this inner circle. The networks, though, don't make decisions for individuals, but function on each and every member's ability to read the group's consensus and stay with the majority. Admission into the network depends on having something to offer, be it knowledge, market information or exploitable connections. You don't join them — they find you and then induct you to the group.

Collectively, these players know the system, the technology, the rules; and they know when to wait, when to move and when to keep quiet. I suspect they come to the meetings to find out what the rest of us do and how we think. You never know — there might be an opportunity. Like the hyenas lurking close by the deer, these self-styled market professionals are always on top of what the mum and dad investors are thinking and doing.

The wise old owl

To complete the analogy, as well as the market novices and shrewd traders, there are also the wise owls. Jan is a divorced baby boomer, a savvy business woman and a long-term investor. Jan is like an owl, sitting up in a tall tree and watching from a safe distance. Decades in the market have sharpened her skills, and the tactics she employs are unique to her long-term objectives. She remains completely unaffected by day-to-day share price movements, as she thinks and operates in a monthly to yearly timeframe. A fast decision for her means having to make up her mind before the month is out. She knows the importance of decision-making and is well aware that hesitation in the stock market is expensive in any timeframe. No doubt she sympathises with the position that Douglas now finds himself in.

The owl, like the driver, wills the deer to move as the final outcome becomes increasingly obvious. The deer's hesitation has seriously reduced its chances of survival. The owl hoots and looks down at its chest, as if resigned to its inability to help. This nocturnal, winged creature is of a different world, where different rules apply. Not a world without danger, but one where predators and prey are armed with different weaponry, designed for a different set of circumstances. The owl can rest easy in the tall tree knowing that it is removed from the world below. About the only common ground it shares with earthbound animals is its ultimate objective of survival.

It's not about being right

The reason for Douglas's inability to make investment decisions, despite his growing knowledge and experience, is in large part because he is afraid of being wrong. That explains why he takes up so much of everyone's time in the Traders Club meetings—if his self-esteem is damaged or he loses money, he has others to blame for his decisions, me not least of all! After all, it's my Traders Club.

But in the marketplace Douglas's choices will diminish quickly with the passage of time, not unlike the deer's. As if triggered by a starting pistol, two of the hyenas sprint across the road behind the deer and cut off any chance of escape in the opposite direction. The owl, as if responding to a dramatic climax in a movie, suddenly lifts and starts to bring its wings up, only to settle back on its perch. The inevitability of the outcome has hit all of those present. The hyenas collectively rise up from their crouching positions, tails relaxed. The deer's small body loses its tension and it shifts its gaze to the windshield as if to plead with the semi-trailer, 'You have the power—please stop'.

The driver feels a sting of guilt as he double-clutches down and guns the engine. He knows that if he and his truck weren't on the road this macabre theatre wouldn't be taking place. But although his presence is not an act of nature, he too is performing a function that is linked to his survival. The owl blinks and looks up into the night sky, as if unable to watch the final act.

The truck passes by with building speed as if exiting the stage. The hyenas trot forward to the still warm carcass in a casual, unhurried manner. Roadkill is a favourite because the truck, unlike lions, leaves them the entire carcass and poses no lingering threat. The incursion of man and machine into their world has introduced an opportunity for reward that carries reduced risk. But they must adapt to this new opportunity by keeping a watchful eye on the roads.

Back to Douglas. I offer him a last-ditch escape: 'You could put it in the bottom drawer'. I say it with a grin and the tension washes from the room. Jan, who's been glaring at Harold the whole time, finally looks away from him but she's still not smiling. Everyone knows that I'm offering Douglas a poor, virtually unacceptable answer, but it's the only way he can get back into his seat and become part of the group again. He takes the bait but plays politics with his answer, 'Unless you can offer a better alternative?' One of the traders rolls his eyes as Douglas takes his seat. I grin and give him some added dignity by announcing that I don't necessarily know the right answer either.

The meeting continues and I look in Douglas's direction to observe him with his head down, staring at the back of the chair in front of him. He knows that by his own volition he's condemned himself to a life of passive investing. A harsh reality given that his original intention was to be an active investor.

For every 'Douglas' who learns to survive, there will be another dozen 'Douglases' who fall by the wayside. It may seem that this man-made machine known as the marketplace doesn't want the newcomer to know the rules. Maybe the machine needs victims to feed its insatiable appetite?

It's the ability to make a decision and cop the consequences that counts. It is not the ability to make the right decisions—that comes with time. Provided, of course that it's YOU making the decisions. The lesson you learnt in school where a wrong decision was considered bad doesn't apply in the marketplace. The newcomer certainly has to gain knowledge, but it should be born of a real need for answers and not a desire to be right all the time.

For Douglas to survive and thrive in the marketplace instead of becoming roadkill, he needs to alter his perspective. To help him do this we have to go back to the beginning of the whole process. Not to the initial, well-intentioned discussion with his wife about their financial future where they decided to build a prison of knowledge, but earlier.

Now more than ever

With the advancement of technology and the resulting increased speed with which we do business, the days of the passive investor are numbered. The business world moves faster and faster with the passage of time and, in order to reflect this, financial markets are evolving at an increased rate as well. Even long-term investors are discovering, usually through financial loss, that an active approach to managing your investments is essential in today's environment.

Money not maths

You don't have to have an accounting degree or be an expert at technical analysis to be a successful investor or trader. What you do need is an elementary level of numeracy. This is unavoidable — buying and selling shares requires it. I have included charts throughout to illustrate different concepts and validate the different forms of analysis being used, and no doubt this may lead some readers to accuse me of being more chartist than anything else. While this accusation is probably true, charts contain the only facts that are to be found in the marketplace — historical price data. However, I have kept the use of rocket science to an absolute minimum and assumed that the reader is interested in money, not maths.

Alan Hull
Melbourne
December 2008

Chapter 1

The marketplace

Fact: stockbrokers are not paid to give advice on shares

Before we decide on a plan of attack we must study the game and the rules that govern it. As the name implies, the stock market is a marketplace where shares are bought and sold. Each share effectively represents an infinitesimally small piece of the underlying company. If you own a share in a publicly listed company, then you own an infinitesimally small piece of that company. Anyone can buy and sell shares via the stock market and, thanks largely to the advent of the internet, the cost of dealing in shares, known as brokerage, can be as low as $20.

The stock market, then, is the nucleus of the machine we affectionately refer to as the marketplace and its operation is reasonably straightforward. The complexities occur in the outer shells which cover this simple nucleus. This chapter attempts to demystify these complexities by taking a closer look at some of these outer layers.

The players

Firstly, let's identify the direct users of the stock market and shed some light on their activities. They include among others:

- individual investors
- traders
- speculators
- broking houses
- private and public companies
- managed funds.

This assortment of individual users will probably come as no surprise to you, but it is worthwhile noting the differing timeframes in which they operate. Some work in timeframes as short as 10 minutes, thanks largely to modern technology, while other individuals will hold shares for decades.

Most of us fill the space in between these two extremes. To adopt the view that there is only one workable timeframe would be extremely foolish; a historical study of the longevity of each group would quickly dispel this assertion. However, intra-day trading of any kind is yet to establish a proven track record, given that it is a function of only recent technological advances.

Initial public offering

The picture gets more interesting as we start to look at the larger users—corporate and institutional buyers and sellers of shares. If you're a private company wanting to list on a stock exchange and you wish to issue millions of shares in your company to raise working capital, then someone's going to have to sell those shares. You would employ the services of a stockbroking house to promote your new shares and orchestrate your 'initial public offering' (or IPO), this being the first appearance of your shares in the marketplace.

The broker receives a substantial fee for their services and is keen to obtain such business, particularly when a market boom is underway and shiny new shares with a lot of promise are easy to sell. The ultimate

IPO for stockbrokers in recent times would have been the floating of Telstra, which was well-received by investors. Unfortunately, the second tranche of shares, T-2, didn't end in as favourable an outcome for investors, but that didn't harm enthusiasm for the final float, T-3, which was considered a resounding success.

Stockbrokers can be caught out if things don't go as planned because their end of the deal is to underwrite the issuing of shares being offered by the would-be public company. So if any shares aren't issued, the stockbroker picks up the tab at a previously agreed price. Hence the stockbroker is also a direct user of the stock market. This underwriting puts the stockbroker under considerable pressure to sell the shares, while alleviating uncertainty for the company.

Having had to deal with this pressure over the years, stockbrokers have turned the process of issuing new shares into an art form. Prior to the shares being traded on the stock market, the stockbroker offers allocations of shares to its private clients, with several stockbroking firms being able to offer allocations of shares in the same company at the same time. This adds another dimension to the whole process as it now pays for you and me to be a client of a stockbroker who can offer us an allocation of shares at the issue price prior to their initial listing on the exchange. It is our hope that the issue price we pay is at a discount to the price that the shares are likely to fetch in the open marketplace. Stockbrokers use this 'exclusive access' to share issues as a marketing tool.

Stockbrokers may also hold an 'off-market bulk-buy discount sale', also known as an institutional book build. Institutional investors get a bite of the cherry at a discounted price, providing they purchase substantial blocks of the shares on offer. This book-building process is a win-win situation for both parties. Depending on the demand for the new shares, the stockbroker will pre-allocate a certain number of shares to be made available to private clients with the remainder going to the institutional book build.

As you can see, stockbrokers are doing a balancing act between getting the best possible price for the shares and not being caught out with any left unissued. If there are shares left over then the stockbroker will sell them into the open marketplace after the initial listing. You can see how the resources boom that peaked in 2007 was of great benefit to all concerned. Stockbrokers couldn't get enough IPOs on the books to meet the demand that you and I placed on them for share allocations in resource and energy stocks, and the mining companies were lining up to get their hands on more working capital.

Raising working capital

Private companies benefit in other ways as well. Let's pretend that you're a partner in a privately owned company that provides services to the mining sector. A commodities boom is underway and everyone in the marketplace is trying to sell you and your partners on the idea of going public and listing on the stock market. You are reluctant to list because the idea of losing control is abhorrent to you, but you decide to play along anyway on the proviso that you and your original partners retain the balance of power in the boardroom. After all, more working capital never hurt anyone!

You value your company at $2 million in assets and a further $10 million in goodwill. The goodwill is based on your existing earnings plus projected earnings growth using an exponential curve approach. Figure 1.1 shows a comparison over time between a straight line, indicating constant earnings growth, and an exponential curve that represents accelerating growth.

Figure 1.1: earnings graph

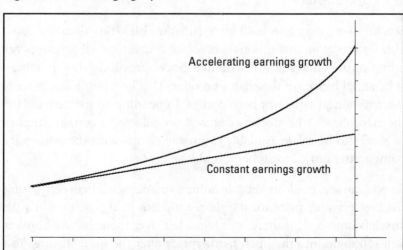

You will have to make a good case for using an exponential earnings growth curve to gain the approval of the Australian Securities & Investments Commission (ASIC), who must rubber stamp your prospectus prior to you listing on the stock exchange. You will also be setting up your prospectus with the assistance of the stockbroker who is, in effect, selling your prospectus to the marketplace. Your supporting argument might be similar to that shown in table 1.1.

Table 1.1: figures supporting accelerating earnings growth

Year	Earnings	Earnings growth (%)
2003a	$50 000	—
2004a	$55 000	10
2005a	$63 000	15
2006a	$77 000	22
2007a	$95 000	34

You're understandably reluctant to rock the boat by going public because you've just got your business to the point where all the partners are drawing a wage and receiving their share of $95 000 in profits. You could slow down and still achieve growth. But wait—there's more (see table 1.2).

Table 1.2: projected earnings

Year	Projected earnings	Projected earnings growth (%)
2008p	$143 000	51
2009p	$239 000	67

The years with an 'a' next to them are where you know the 'actual' figures, whereas the 'p' stands for 'projected'. The projected figures come from projecting earnings growth into the future. Because nobody knows the full potential of the current boom you can't set the ceiling for earnings growth. But you can do your best by using third-party statistics that infer conclusions from the current rate of growth in mainland China and the demand this is creating for the resource companies you provide services to.

You are diligent in this process and, with the help of the working capital you're going to raise, you intend to expand overseas. Your statistics reflect this intention and you receive your rubber stamp. You're happy, the broker's happy and the public are happy because they're going to get a piece of the action when your projections are realised — if that ever happens.

You retain control of your company because the original partners retain six million shares issued at $1 each between them, with the other five million shares sold outside the company. The day of the IPO arrives and the share price closes at $1.50 having been as high as $2.00 during trading. You sit down and do some calculations to realise that you're now a millionaire.

It suddenly dawns on you why they drink champagne on the floor of the ASX during initial listings. You always wondered why company directors got so excited about getting more working capital. Now you know. Your choices are to expand your company overseas and be answerable to thousands of shareholders for your actions or sell your holdings. Having been reluctant to go public in the first place you decide to sell and take the profits. After all, if you still want to work then you can probably get your mates, who are still in control of the company, to hire you back as a consultant.

Raising capital again and again

Existing public companies are also direct users of the marketplace as it provides them with a mechanism to raise additional working capital, acquire other companies, and so on. They raise additional working capital by issuing more shares and effectively going through the float process all over again. They need shareholder approval to do this as it can have a diluting affect on the share price, depending on the reaction of the marketplace. The company is in effect proposing an increase in the supply of shares to the marketplace and if the demand for them doesn't meet the increased supply the share price will fall accordingly.

Companies try to avoid this diluting affect by demonstrating to the marketplace what their improved future prospects will be, should they obtain the capital required to implement new strategies. A company has several options when it comes to issuing additional shares. It can offer the new shares to the general public, to institutional investors, to other companies where a strategic alliance would be mutually beneficial or to existing shareholders. And yes, you guessed it, back to the stockbroker.

As the conversion of shares to cash is a very direct process, it is possible for public companies to use retained shares as a form of currency. They can use their shares to buy other public companies, providing they have the approval of the majority of shareholders. Let's look at the example of a mining company that wants to acquire control of a transport/logistics company so it can reduce its overheads. As seen in table 1.3, at the start of the resources boom both companies have the same market capitalisation, that is, the value of their shares and the number on issue is identical. (Market capitalisation is equal to the value of shares multiplied by the number of shares.)

Table 1.3: market capitalisation at the start of the resources boom

	Mining company	Transport company
Market capitalisation	$10 million	$10 million

The resources boom then starts to take effect on the mining company's share price but has only a marginal impact on the share price of the transport company. The market now values the mining company at four times the value of the transport company (see table 1.4).

Table 1.4: market capitalisation during the resources boom

	Mining company	Transport company
Market capitalisation	$48 million	$12 million

The mining company's board of directors gets together and starts to discuss its options. As you can probably guess, this is going to be a lengthy meeting due to the number of possibilities that need to be considered. Do they use shares held by the company, have a share issue, pay cash, attempt a complete takeover or just gain majority control? Of course, they could also combine any number of these options. Understandably they are all quite giddy about the possibilities and it takes them a long time to get to the really big question: who's going to ring the broker?

Advisers, experts and critics

The complexities that we face in dealing with the direct users of the stock market have given birth to yet another layer of complexity. Keep in mind that this newest layer has evolved from our desire to not have to deal with the underlying layer. It is the world of advisers, experts, critics and gurus. Their sole purpose is to comprehend what we don't want to and translate their understanding into meaningful guidance or, to put it more succinctly, money in our pockets. Notice that I wrote 'we don't want to' and not, 'we can't' in the previous sentence. The guiding lights of the marketplace come in many different shapes and sizes including financial planners, investment advisers, market commentators and analysts, trading system vendors and more. This group of helpers has a significant role in the marketplace, and it pays to get to know them.

Financial planners and investment advisers ... are very similar.

Financial planners and investment advisers, in my experience, are very similar. On that basis, I will share one of my early encounters with a financial adviser. At the tender age of 20, just months shy of my 21st birthday, I received a phone call from a man who said he was a financial adviser and that he would like to set up a consultation with me to discuss my financial future. It was at no cost to me, and he was extremely flexible as to where and when the consultation would take place.

Due in large part to his apparently altruistic intentions and concern for my future welfare, I agreed to meet him. At the time of the consultation I found myself in the presence of a tallish man, dressed in a very impressive double-breasted three-piece suit, sporting just a touch of grey at his sideburns and wearing a friendly, obliging grin. Having just left home and the watchful eye of my parents, my first thought was, 'How lucky am I?' Here was this obviously important man, to whom I warmed immediately, who was going to look after me by taking care of my financial future while I worried about more immediate problems such as cars and girls. He asked me, in an authoritative tone, if I had a superannuation policy. It was, he explained, vital to my future wellbeing at retirement. He added that all sensible and mature people who didn't want to become a burden on their friends and family in retirement had one. He then handed me a document containing national statistics on the ageing population, proving that reliance on the pension in retirement would be futile.

Fear shot through me as I realised that I couldn't even spell 'suporanuation' and I felt my face flush with embarrassment. Add to this my shame at the thought of being a burden on my loved ones in the future and my confusion at the word 'demographic' written on the piece of paper in my hand. I'd been on my own in the big bad world for a brief few months and look at the damage I might have caused simply by not knowing about something like 'suporanuation'. I uttered in a whimper, 'What should I do?'

Luckily, he had prepared an important-looking document with my name at the top of each page that contained the most fantastic news. If I contributed just $700 a year, BEFORE TAX SO I WOULDN'T EVEN FEEL IT, to a superannuation fund then I would have over $300 000 to play with in retirement. Well, I nearly kissed the man as I realised that not only had I avoided financial Armageddon, but I was going to have enough money to help others in retirement.

The tone of the meeting had relaxed, as you tend to do just after a near-death experience, when he asked me with a hint of concern in his voice when my 21st birthday was. My eyes widened and the stiffness returned to my body as I replied, 'In two months … is that a problem?' With parental-like concern he explained to me that it was necessary I start the policy before I turned 21. With this revelation I nearly climbed into his lap, trying to get my hands on the super policy that would change my life back to what it had been the day before.

While this anecdote is based on real events in my life, I have exaggerated it for the purpose of illustrating several key points. Firstly, I was dealing with a salesperson and not someone with purely altruistic intentions. I do recall wondering at the time as to why he required no payment for his services. Curiously, several of my friends were also approached just before their 21st birthdays.

Now to the policy in question. The lesson here, in advance, is to read the fine print. The short version is that the printout I was shown containing figures that would have made Donald Trump drool at the time, bore scant resemblance to the actual performance of the policy. It was based on a 15 per cent annual interest rate compounding over 40 years.

My contributions, included in the equation, started at $700 per annum but increased over time in line with the consumer price index (CPI) figure. The 15 per cent annual growth figure used reflected the current performance of the superannuation fund at that time. Like most individuals enjoying their twenties, I left the superannuation policy in the bottom drawer and went about my life, comfortable in the knowledge it was there.

After 10 years of dutifully making the compulsory contributions to the fund and now having the option of not making any more, I decided to fish out the policy and original printout to see if I was still on target for my villa in the Bahamas. This action was also prompted, in part, by the constant increases to the annual contributions, which were becoming a perpetual annoyance. You can imagine my surprise when the actual performance of the fund, according to my annual statement, was approximately half the projected figure on the original printout. Finding the relevant figures among the reams of paper sent to me each year was no mean feat, either.

I will demonstrate in simple form what happened to me, and the power of compound interest. Table 1.5 shows the difference between the guaranteed performance of the fund and the performance shown on the original printout using 15 per cent. For simplicity I have excluded my contributions and the fund administration fees and used a starting figure of $1000.

Table 1.5: guaranteed versus projected fund performance over 10 years

Year	Guaranteed performance (9%)	Projected performance (15%)
1	$1090	$1150
2	$1188	$1322

Year	Guaranteed performance (9%)	Projected performance (15%)
3	$1295	$1521
4	$1412	$1749
5	$1539	$2011
6	$1677	$2313
7	$1828	$2660
8	$1992	$3059
9	$2172	$3518
10	$2367	$4046

The interest rate is critical when you are compounding it over time. Figure 1.2 illustrates the difference between nine and 15 per cent per annum when compounded over an entire working life.

Figure 1.2: comparison between 9 per cent and 15 per cent annual returns when compounded over 40 years

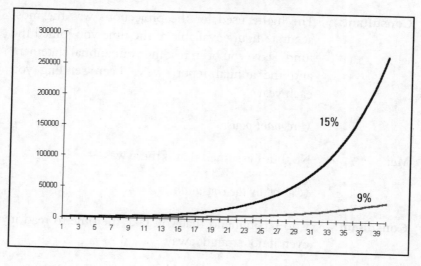

If I continued the table for another 30 years to my eagerly anticipated retirement at age 60, the resulting figures would be as shown in table 1.6 (overleaf).

Table 1.6: guaranteed versus projected fund performance after 40 years

Year	Guaranteed performance (9%)	Projected performance (15%)
40	$31 409	$267 863

Of course my figures were muddied by other factors such as my annual contributions, the actual CPI, increases to the administration fees and the actual performance of the fund. However, I was looking at a similar scenario when, as if by magic, I found myself with the phone at my ear, dialing a number that had also been buried in the reams of paper. I had prepared a couple of confronting questions and the conversation went something like this:

Me: The growth of the fund doesn't match the figure used on the printout I was shown when I joined the fund. What's the story?

Consultant: The figure used for the projections was the most accurate figure available at the time you joined the fund. Have you been reading your annual statement and the annual report we've been sending you each year?

(Pregnant pause)

Me: No, but I assumed that if there was—

(Cut off by the consultant)

Consultant: I do recommend that you take the time to read it, even if not straight away.

Me: *(With an incredulous tone in my voice)*

So you're telling me, if I don't have enough money to retire, it's my fault because I haven't read the material you sent me? Surely there's some kind of guarantee on the fund's performance?

Consultant:	(*With an indignant tone in her voice*)
	Of course there is. It's in your original policy document. Haven't you read that either?
Me:	(*With the sudden realisation that I'd been staring at the headlights of an oncoming truck all these years*)
	No.
Consultant:	(*Resigned to the inevitability of the situation, the consultant double-clutches down and guns the engine*)
	I SUGGEST THAT YOU READ IT AND THEN CALL ME BACK.

Needless to say, my embarrassment was so great I never rang back. Now we get to the reams of paper that were delivered annually to my letterbox, and the original policy document I'd neglected to read in the first place. It was all there in black and white: the minimum annual growth guarantee of nine per cent, notification of changes in administration fees for the forthcoming period and changes to my contributions based on the CPI, including a complete explanation of the calculation being employed. By burying it all in the proverbial bottom drawer, I hadn't lost a single cent. Indeed, I was actually showing a small profit, but I felt the loss of 10 wasted years.

Managed funds

When shopping for a babysitter for your money several options are available. You can let a financial consultant, by whatever name, do it all for you, or you can choose your own managed fund and still avoid being a direct user of the marketplace. The financial papers carry large ads expounding the virtues of a wide range of investment products from a variety of different institutions.

The marketing tactics employed in these ads are not dissimilar to the tactics employed elsewhere, where advertisers attempt to sell through fear, social pressure, authority, scarcity and so on. Most of these tactics exploit the fact we're very busy in modern life and seeking short cuts.

An example of social pressure is a financial institution that uses most of its advertising space expounding on how many countries it has offices in and the fact it has 20 million customers worldwide.

Your thinking goes, 'If 20 million other people have done their homework and they all agree, who am I to argue?' You go with the consensus of the group because that will save you having to conduct your own investigations. International equity funds use the scarcity tactic by telling you how insignificant the Australian marketplace is on a global scale, and that if you don't have offshore exposure then you're missing out on most of the action. At the expense of personal embarrassment I think I've already covered fear and authority.

But one common tactic that never ceases to amaze me is the use of tax deductibility to sell investment products. While I don't dismiss the importance of the tax issue, I liken this tactic to selling a car by showing customers the fuel economy figures and not the car itself. Fuel economy is important, but don't you think it would be a good idea to see the car first? If you're shopping for an investment product then you're shopping for growth first and possible tax savings second. It's easy to cross these over as both can mean money in your pocket.

Always remember that everyone's tax situation is different and never accept general statements from someone who doesn't know your personal circumstances. Translated this means to always check the tax deductibility of a potential investment with your own accountant. He or she should also make sure that the Australian Taxation Office (ATO) has given the investment product its stamp of approval. In summary, your funds manager is in charge of your investments and your accountant is in charge of your tax liabilities and deductions. Let them liaise with each other but don't let them switch roles. Never forget that a funds manager's job is to get you the best possible return, not to save you tax.

... always check the tax deductibility... with your own accountant.

Now let's return to the reams of paper and my new hobby of reading fine print. Coming forward in time to a recent example, I will show you how this hobby can be very entertaining and enlightening. It was a Saturday morning and I had the business section in front of me and a cup of coffee in my hand. I read my fill of the articles and then began scanning the ads, as is my habit.

I was tiring of the whole process and ready to reach for the motoring section when the most amazing ad caught my eye (see figure 1.3). Details have been altered to protect against litigation from the company which is, incidentally, larger than the public service of most developing nations. What's more, I have only included the details I deem relevant.

Figure 1.3: advertisement example

Capital

20% Guaranteed⁺

Acme Australian Equity Fund

* Annualised compound interest over the three year period from 1/1/2005 through to 1/1/2008 and 20 per cent is based on all growth being reinvested over the period specified — past results are no guarantee of future performance.

+ Capital guarantee by third-party underwriter and exercisable at the completion of the term at 31/1/2010.

My eyes widened and my jaw dropped at '20% Guaranteed' but I quickly regained my composure to read the small print. Let me translate what this ad is actually saying. We'll deal with the *capital* guarantee first. This guarantee covers your initial investment capital and not the 20 per cent return. But here's the kicker: you can only reclaim your original investment at the end of the investment term, which is the end of 2010 — and this ad appeared in mid 2008.

So the worst scenario the fund is looking at is an interest-free loan of your money for the intervening two-and-a-half-year period. Basically, you get your money back but you've wasted your time. The next point to note is that the 20 per cent is annualised compound interest. This means that they have applied the compound principle to calculate this figure.

For example, let's assume that you originally invested $1000 in the fund. The 20 per cent annualised compound interest means that your initial investment has grown 20 per cent per year using the compound affect. This is shown in table 1.7 (overleaf).

Table 1.7: investment growth using compound interest

Year	20% annualised compound interest	20% annual interest
1	$1200	$1200
2	$1400	$1440
3	$1600	$1728

If you thought you were going to do the compounding, think again. In terms of the actual return you're down from a 73 per cent return on investment to 60 per cent. Of course the reason why funds publish the compounded figure is because it is higher than the average simple annual return. We can, however, work out how they have performed on an annual return basis, as shown in table 1.8.

Table 1.8: the actual percentage growth

Year	Investment value	Growth
1	$1170	17%
2	$1369	17%
3	$1602	17%

The 20 per cent is calculated by dividing the return over the entire period by the term of the period. Has there been a deception? Strictly speaking, no. Is the ad visually deceptive? That's a matter of opinion. This is why it *does* pay to have a good investment adviser. If you are shopping for a managed fund yourself, make sure you understand the difference between annual interest, which can be compounded, and annualised compound interest, which has already been compounded.

It also pays to check for consistency over the lifetime of a fund. I once found an Asian equity fund that returned 38 per cent in one year but returned only 12 per cent on average over three years. It was simply in the right place at the right time. As with any other commercial enterprise, promoters of managed funds will put their best foot forward when it comes to advertising and marketing. Unfortunately, investors have to take returns from the best years *and* the bad years.

Armed with information

Those of us who want to have more direct control over our investments and be better informed about the marketplace have a plethora of options when it comes to getting our hands on information and informed opinion. We have television, radio, newspapers, investment clubs, the internet, seminars, books, research analysts who work for stockbroking houses, magazines and more.

Through this range of media we have access to both factual information and opinions from a variety of experts who specialise in an array of fields. Their combined expertise covers economics, specific industry sectors, local and foreign financial markets, taxation, shares, companies, debt management, politics, currencies, commodities, cyclical analysis, technical analysis, fundamental analysis, managed funds, futures contracts, options, contracts for difference (CFDs), warrants, superannuation, pensions and annuities, just to name a few.

These experts can, and often do, offer opposing opinions and the number of experts also continues to grow. Unfortunately I don't have a Cray computer to calculate the number of permutations of media and experts there are but by the time I'd worked it out, it would be invalid anyway. However, I do know that the number is such that I can't absorb and assimilate all of the information and opinions on offer. Bear in mind that the information overload is created by our own desire to be better informed on the back of someone else's expertise.

Being human, of course, we will take the obvious short cut to deal with the problem. We decide on a favourite medium such as a particular magazine. We subscribe to it religiously and avidly follow a particular expert commentator's opinion. Until the inevitable happens, then the realisation we have misplaced our faith sinks in. We then go in search of another expert and a new home for our faith.

Enter Big Brother

Regardless of who gives us advice or which market commentators we listen to, the one constant is the regulators, collectively known as Big

Brother. Big Brother is omnipresent and is watching the marketplace from several vantage points. ASIC polices, in association with the Australian Securities Exchange (ASX), the activities of private and publicly owned companies, everyone who buys and sells shares, everyone who gives advice on buying and selling shares and all managed funds.

In its job of policing publicly listed companies it receives aid and assistance from the Australian Competition and Consumer Commission (ACCC), which keeps a watchful eye over the interests of consumers. An example of the ACCC's power is the ability to block a merger between any two companies if the merger is deemed to be detrimental to the interests of the general public. While it is my opinion that the ASX is not entirely impartial, given that it is itself a publicly listed company and therefore has a commercial agenda, Big Brother does the best job it can. However, keep in mind that the police usually show up at the scene of a crime and not before. The only cure for losing money is to get it back, not a shoulder to cry on.

The only cure for losing money is to get it back, not a shoulder to cry on.

The best analogy to describe the marketplace in its entirety is to compare it to the hallowed turf of the MCG after an Aussie rules football match. In days gone by you could go onto the ground when the game was over and this created some rare sights. Watching people playing kick-to-kick from the fence line, you would see what appeared to be a confused swarm of footballs flying overhead. As soon as one fell earthward, another one would be kicked up to take its place. The swarm never rested and you'd get the impression that a large unstoppable force was at work.

As you looked horizontally across the ground, all you'd see is the small group of people playing kick-to-kick right in front of you. When I first witnessed this phenomenon I quickly realised I wasn't taking in the whole scene and went up to the top of the stand to take another look. Watching from an elevated vantage point, I stood in awe of the magnitude of the scene in front of me. There were children and adults kicking footballs, people crossing the ground purposefully, others just idly standing about, policemen dotted around the fringes looking in, and many others. But the magnitude was lost, save for the swarm of footballs, when I went back down to join the throng.

Strolling around the ground you're struck by a different phenomenon. Each person or group of people appears to be totally self-absorbed and operating independently of everyone else. All of them have a purpose in being on the ground and contribute to the swarm effect, but they seem oblivious to all the other people around them. Then suddenly you became aware of the danger from the swarm of footballs above you. Badly aimed kicks mean that if you're not concentrating skyward, you're likely to be struck by a stray Sherrin. But then again, if you love the game, you accept the danger.

Chapter 2

The evolution of the marketplace

We always get what we need out of life,
but not necessarily what we want

We will gain a better understanding of the marketplace if we focus our attention on the objectives of the participants, rather than our perception of their function. Both private and public companies are looking out for their own interests and that of their shareholders; the higher their share price is, the better. If you listen to the CEO of a publicly listed company being interviewed, you will notice that he chooses his words to paint his company in the best possible light.

If you want an unbiased opinion, then listen to the media commentators or funds managers. It's in their interests to give the facts, regardless of the impact this will have on the company. Personally, I ignore reports from research analysts who are employed by stockbrokers. Stockbrokers work for the companies, as well as us, and their in-house analysts are unlikely to present a critical report on one of their own clients. Imagine the call from your broker: 'We can get you a share allocation for Acme Mining but our chief analyst's report recommends not taking it because the projections in the prospectus are far too optimistic. Are you interested?'

In the beginning

The first stockbroker was a salesperson employed by a business manager to help raise capital to grow their business. Somewhere down the line another stockbroker must have become sick and tired of searching for would-be investors. So he decided to have potential investors at his fingertips and in order to do this, he needed a marketing tool. This, of course, was his knowledge of the companies, and so he became an investment adviser.

From this point on, the stockbroker was working both sides of the street. Therefore, to see stockbroking in its true light, we must firstly get the notion out of our heads that stockbrokers exist solely for our benefit. Stockbroking is a business and, like the rest of us, stockbrokers need to earn a living. Like the hyena I talked about in the preface, stockbrokers are opportunistic and unlikely to change their ways in the foreseeable future.

But at some point in history the investors, using their combined voting power, gave Big Brother a wake up call. They told Big Brother that the stockbrokers were working both sides of the street and needed an umpire. The Securities Commission was then created to keep everyone in line.

The rules that govern the marketplace are in a constant state of flux in an effort to keep up with changes. For example, one of Big Brother's recent challenges is the advent of the internet and how to govern it effectively given its lack of geographical boundaries.

An unwanted side effect of regulation is that the legal complexities and liabilities associated with stockbroking have reached the point where a broker's education is dominated by the need to understand the legal ramifications of giving advice rather than what advice to give. In an ideal world stockbrokers would be paid for the advice they give, not use it as a marketing tool, and they would be properly trained to give it.

We want the governing bodies to protect our interests, but we don't like it when they make the stockbroker's job harder or when innovative corporate strategies are blocked. In summary, no-one likes the umpire but we all need one.

Back to the history lesson. The now wary investors, who weren't happy with the free advice from their stockbrokers, wanted other ways of finding good investments. More to the point, they wanted someone to do it for them. Enter the investment adviser.

The history of investment advisers

Although history doesn't support me in this, I suspect the first investment adviser was stoned to death by his own clients, which is a tragedy because he probably knew something about investing in the stock market. My theory on the evolution of investment advisers is that many now call themselves funds managers and are several layers removed from the general public. This theory is largely based on the fact that I have never met a funds manager in person (other than myself). They still perform the original function of investing other people's money in the stock market and other investment media, but they do so from a safe distance. Their services are available to us through intermediaries known as financial advisers, financial planners and modern investment advisers. The expertise of this group is very broad and, like stockbrokers, their training focuses mainly on the legalities of their job.

The Securities Commission was ... created to keep everyone in line.

In a manner similar to stockbrokers, investment advisers have evolved from the role of salesperson in the employ of managed funds. They will analyse your personal financial circumstances and make investment recommendations, the idea being that your risk profile, tax situation, personal objectives, and so on, will be taken into account when they develop an investment strategy for you. The regulations and disclosure rules governing this group of advisers have been tightened in recent years to ensure they act in the best interests of the public and not for their own gain. This is because their income is largely derived from the commissions they are paid from the managed funds and not from us, their clients.

It should also be noted that funds managers derive their income from the administration fees they charge us. In most cases these fees are based on the amount of money under management and not on the actual performance of the fund. Of course, the performance of the fund is indirectly linked to the funds manager's income as they will be unable to attract investors to their fund if it's performing badly.

Do-it-yourself

The media and other information vendors are deriving income from meeting the needs of those of us who want to be more hands-on in the stock market. They continually find new and exciting ways of supplying information to us with the help of modern technology. Their income is derived from the sale of their respective information services and they are generally unbiased with respect to the content they're providing.

Included in this group are organisations and individuals such as myself, who aim to educate prospective stock market participants. While we all provide raw information to the public, we also sell methods and strategies for using that information. You can pay for an abundance of courses, books, computer programs and so on, that will teach you how to trade and invest in shares.

In addition, newspapers and magazines carry articles by journalists who offer various opinions based on their respective areas of expertise. While everyone in this group is paid directly for their services, unlike stockbrokers and funds managers, the sheer volume of product they supply has crippled the consumer. The original problem of indecision has been exacerbated, rather than solved, by the arrival of the information revolution.

After 15 years of working in the technology industry, I can sympathise with anyone who finds themselves more, rather than less, perplexed by the increasing number of options on offer. As an electronic technician, every time a company upgraded the design of a computer, printer, modem, and so forth, I had to go back to school. You'll probably be gratified to know that many of the people working in technology-related industries haven't got a clear understanding of the latest technology either. We used to joke that the difference between a used car salesman and a computer salesman was that the used car salesman knew when he was lying.

Misunderstanding and misuse of technology starts at the most basic conceptual level. Put simply, technology should enhance our ability to meet our needs. It is a means to an end and not an end in itself. Problems start when the advancement of technology is driven by forces other than our needs. In short, if it isn't broken, don't fix it but if it's causing you pain, get rid of it.

Technology must be seen as a tool. As a person who used to derive an income from using such tools, I know that they should be simple, unbreakable and appropriate to the job. If they are complicated, then they are a hindrance. If they are unreliable, then they will cost me money. And if I use the wrong tool, then I am wasting my time.

The technological evolution of the everyday family car is a good example of technology being driven by need. Cars, through the use of highly sophisticated technology are, from the consumer's perspective, becoming simpler by the model. Years ago we had to use a choke to start our cars, warm them up for five minutes, change gears using a clutch pedal, avoid leaving the headlights on and remember to get a regular service. Today my car has no choke, doesn't require the use of the throttle to get it started, needs no warm-up time, has an automatic gearshift, and it tells me when I've left the headlights on or it needs a service.

The only thing I have to do is know how to drive it where I need to go and even this task is easier with the advent of satellite navigation systems. An 'engine management system' under the bonnet is doing all the work for me. What's more, I have no idea how it works or how to program it. This is the correct application of technology.

Banks, on the other hand, have employed modern technology to reduce their overheads, rather than to provide improved services for their customers. If we use ATMs instead of bank tellers, then the banks can close branches and retrench the many staff that are needed to run them. In fact, the banking industry is a major beneficiary of digital communication. Its stock-in-trade, money, can now be transferred via copper wire.

Of course we are told through their marketing campaigns that these advances are for our benefit. But the proof of the pudding is in the eating, or in this case, banking. Having developed systems that meet their needs rather than those of the consumer, banks are now facing a customer backlash against changes to the system.

In a similar vein, electronic receptionists who answer the phone with a pre-recorded series of options aren't really there to make the consumer's life easier. Electronic receptionists are of benefit to the company that employs them by reducing their staff costs, but are an annoyance to most callers. When first introduced they were promoted as a benefit to customers who never wanted them in the first place. If these technological changes were really meant to be for our benefit, then someone is very wide off the mark.

Technology for investors

This use and misuse of technology relates back to us as investors. Because we have ready access to an ocean of market information, we tend to make choices that aren't based on our needs. We soak up electronically transmitted information without realising that it is doing us more harm than good by increasing the number of variables we have to deal with. Going onto the internet without purpose can be not only a waste of time and energy, but can also make us over-informed investors.

Our attitude towards the marketplace is the difference between success and failure. The majority of people, with the encouragement of service and product suppliers, behave like children let loose in a lolly shop, indiscriminately buying products and services as if they were objects of a child's desire. The marketplace is of our own making but it has the ability to roll right over the top of us if we're not careful. We must be very selective when it comes to paying for information and advice.

The appeal of advice

Having read this far, you will have realised there is plenty of advice to be had. In many instances, it's offered without you even having asked a question. So what is the great appeal of advice to us, the consumer? The short answer is that it's a short cut.

If we act on someone else's advice we can save a lot of time and effort. Unfortunately, most people are under the misguided impression that seeking advice is a substitute for decision-making. While professional advisers have a duty of care to ensure the advice they give us is correct, ultimately they are not responsible for the resulting decisions that you and I make.

If we look around us we will see that successful people don't pay for advice, they pay for answers. What's more, they only pay for answers if finding their own would be too time-consuming. The difference between successful and unsuccessful investors is that the former have specific questions that need answering, while the latter don't have any beyond, 'How do I make money from shares?' A classic example of this is the very first phone call a newcomer makes to their stockbroker. They start by acknowledging the broker's authority and admitting they doen't even know what they want. Their opening line is, 'I'm new to the stock market and I don't really know anything about it so I'm open to whatever you suggest'. The stockbroker has just secured the newcomer's patronage on the false assumption by the newcomer that the broker is going to make their decisions for them.

Our attitude towards the marketplace is the difference between success and failure.

Note the words that are used by all who give advice to others: 'That's my advice but it's your decision'. There is a duty of care to give the correct advice but the responsibility for the outcome goes with the decision. Do not underestimate the importance of this distinction.

Meeting our needs

People usually come into the market with a desire to make money rather than the need to make money. This apparently subtle difference in our approach to the marketplace means that we don't have specific needs or questions that require answers. Advice-givers will say en masse that the most difficult aspect of their job is identifying people's needs. This brings us to the quintessential difference between those who succeed and those who fail.

Our needs come from our responsibilities. Thus the most powerful driving force in my life is my responsibilities. For instance, I need to make money because I need to provide for my family. Baby boomers are my most receptive students because they need to fund their retirement without having to work. On the other hand, people who want to be wealthy will most likely fail. Those who perceive a need to be wealthy tend to be more successful, even if that need comes from simply wanting a bigger house or a new car. It may seem like a fine line between the two but those who are driven to achieve are motivated by real or perceived responsibilities, which the casual observer can often mistake for obsession.

The downside is that responsibilities can also cause heart attacks and damage to our self-esteem if we fail to fulfill them, hence the desire to offload our responsibilities onto others. Responsibilities beget needs, needs beget problems, problems beget answers and from an ocean of information we distil a precious drop of wisdom.

Have you ever known someone who spent their lives dodging responsibility only to find themselves in a very tough corner at some point? Then as if by a miracle, they suddenly emerge from their difficulties a different person. Once responsibility was forced upon them the growing process began. To have wisdom is to possess applicable knowledge which is only obtained by the need to solve problems that are born of our responsibilities. Give someone else your responsibility and you will not obtain wisdom, and this is what the majority of people do in the marketplace.

Unfortunately, responsibility can also bring pain — the pain of failure. In the stock market as with life in general, most people avoid this pain by avoiding responsibility. If I'm not responsible for my actions then I'm not responsible for the failures, so the desire to hand over my responsibility to someone else is very powerful. However, in the stock market if it's your money then it is your responsibility. Any time you try to offload responsibility by seeking advice all you're really doing is handing over the privilege of control.

When someone asks me how I learnt about trading and investing I reply, 'With a very high pain threshold, both financially and psychologically'. To quantify it, I once lost over $30 000 in less than

48 hours. That's a lot of pain if you're prepared to accept responsibility for it. But if I could wind back the clock I wouldn't change it because I would only have made the same mistakes further down the track and probably on a bigger scale. My knowledge in the marketplace is directly proportional to the pain I have suffered at the hands of my own losses. Basically, I am successful because I am prepared to fail.

The stockbroker's responsibilities

While I delegate tasks to others, I never abdicate responsibility for those tasks. In contrast to the newcomer's initial contact with a stockbroker, an experienced market participant's first conversation will go something like this:

- I don't want you to give me advice unless it's in response to a specific question.

- I will place my orders in the morning and I need you to finetune the entries and exits.

- I will be relying on you for timely information on rumours, company announcements, ex-dividend dates, and so forth, particularly with respect to shares I already own.

I hold the stockbroker responsible for carrying out these tasks. If they fail to do so competently, then I'll go shopping for another stockbroker. Next time you're talking to your broker ask them to define the difference between the expectations of novices and those of professionals and then ask them which group they prefer to deal with. They will most likely prefer professionals as they always know exactly where they stand and what their obligations are.

Furthermore, professionals are usually long-term clients who don't blame their broker every time something goes wrong. Market newcomers on the other hand often attribute blame to their broker whenever they lose money. Of course the opposite rarely applies when they make money.

The blaming process is a pain avoidance mechanism because it gives us the escape hatch of claiming diminished or no responsibility. Victims of the 1987 stock market crash will often say, 'It was just bad timing combined with poor advice from my broker'. In other words, they lost money due to a random event coupled with someone else's incompetence. Try to pin them down on a part of the process where they were personally responsible for a decision with a question such as, 'Why did you choose that particular broker?' and once again they'll claim diminished responsibility by replying that, 'A friend recommended him'.

We might feel better psychologically when we believe it's not our fault, but by disassociating our actions from their outcomes we are shutting down the learning process. Time spent in the marketplace doesn't translate into market experience if we do not take responsibility for all of our actions, including our losses. Personally, one of my greatest moments as a trader was the first time I made all my own decisions in executing a trade. I chose the stock, I decided when to buy and when to sell. When I completed the trade I felt a surge of self-confidence similar to the first time I drove a car by myself. I now realise that my education behind the wheel of a car started from that first solo drive and my real education as a trader also started from that first completely self-directed trade. You won't learn how to drive being chauffeur-driven, nor will you learn anything about trading and investing by using the advice of others.

You won't learn ... anything about trading and investing by using the advice of others.

If we want to be successful in the marketplace then we must have a strategy that puts us in the driver's seat where we have full responsibility, and all the authority and control that this carries with it. At this point we are now ready to have that initial discussion about how we are going to approach the marketplace and our plan will be based on our needs and not on our wants.

Chapter 3

Trader or investor?

The only advantage of not having a plan is that
you will never know when you've failed

Our approach to the marketplace is largely dictated by our view
of our own position. If we see ourselves as retail customers on a
spending spree, then the lolly shop approach is the most likely path
we'll follow: a little bit of this, a little bit of that. Many people who go
down this path will phone me and say they are more confused now
than when they began their journey into the marketplace several
months earlier. This is because they have either lost sight of their
initial objectives or they didn't have any to begin with.

The marketplace is dangerous ground for anyone who is wandering
around without purpose. Even the most disciplined individuals can
fall victim to the enticing products and services on offer. We must
have a perspective that will focus on our needs and make us totally
responsible for fulfilling them. The answer can be found by observing
everyone else in the marketplace.

They are all running their own businesses. Successful investors and
traders see themselves as the managers of these businesses, not as

retail customers protected by other people's promises or guarantees. With this businesslike attitude we can now look at other participants in the marketplace with new-found understanding and a clearer insight into their motivations. The primary purpose of being in business is to make a profit. The question is, why choose the stock market if you want to run your own business? Here are some of the key advantages:

- you can work from home and choose your own hours
- there are no advertising costs because you have ready-made customers
- there are no staff to manage or pay
- there is no bricks and mortar infrastructure
- overheads are very low
- you are your own boss.

While the benefits of running your own stock market business are many, there is a catch. If you make a mistake the penalty is immediate financial loss. It's for this reason the stock market is referred to as the school of hard knocks and it pays to be a quick learner. You can see why many service providers have structured their businesses in the way they have. Their mistakes will have a direct impact on your bank account but only an indirect impact on theirs.

If you're ready to accept direct responsibility for running your own stock market business then the first step is to determine what type of business you wish to run. To do this, ask yourself two questions:

- Do I want to deal with shares, publicly listed companies or both?
- Do I want to be to be an investor or a trader?

Shares versus companies

We now have questions that require answers and to start with, we need to understand the difference between shares and the underlying companies they represent. The difference is the crowd; the crowd being the market participants who collectively place a value on companies via their share price.

For example, if there are 10 million shares issued for XYZ company and the shares are trading at $2 each, then the market capitalisation, or the value that the market places on the company, is:

$$10\,000\,000 \text{ shares} \times \$2 = \$20 \text{ million}$$

However, if the share price falls to $1, then the market has halved the value it places on the company as follows:

$$10\,000\,000 \text{ shares} \times \$1 = \$10 \text{ million}$$

The point here, is that the share price can alter without any change in the performance of the underlying company, its management or future prospects. In theory, the value that market participants place on a company and the actual value of the company in terms of its assets and earnings should be one and the same. However, the crowd forms a slippery barrier between the value of the shares and what the company is actually worth.

The crowd may value the shares using factors that have little or nothing to do with the company itself. Although this may seem to be an unwanted complication, it is the very reason for the marketplace's existence. If we could place a value on shares using solid facts then the stock market would cease to exist. You wouldn't pay $60 for a $50 note, nor would you sell a $50 note for $40. Items with a fixed value can't be traded in a marketplace.

Shares are an intangible representation of tangible companies. These two components are linked together via us, the crowd. Although we own public companies by possessing shares in them, it is also important to differentiate between shares and the public companies that they represent.

For example, the 43 per cent collapse in the All Ordinaries index in October 1987 (as shown in figure 3.1 overleaf) was due to the sentiment of the crowd. It had little to do with the actual earning capacity of the underlying companies.

Figure 3.1: All Ordinaries index crash in 1987

Investing versus trading

The next point requiring clarification is the difference between investing and trading. To understand the difference is extremely difficult as investing is defined as applying or using money to create profits and/or devoting time and effort to such an enterprise. One could include, by this definition, any undertaking that involves putting effort into realising either profits or savings. Apart from making the expression 'passive investing' a contradiction in itself, this definition makes everyone present in the marketplace an investor of sorts.

So we will differentiate between investors and traders by coming at the issue from the other end. Traders, by definition, are individuals who buy and sell products for profit. Most of us think of traders as the people who run retail stores selling tangible goods. Stock market traders are doing exactly the same thing, they just don't have retail stores.

Traders are generally perceived as working in a shorter timeframe than investors, but this is a common misconception. Traders themselves are a type of investor. The time that a share is held or the number of buy and sell orders executed by an individual in a given space of time has no bearing on whether they are a trader or an investor.

If we eliminate everyone in the stock market who is buying and selling shares for profit, that is, all the traders, then we are left with the people who use shares or companies as assets. We will define these people as investors.

Our options

Now that we have defined shares, companies, traders and investors we can look at the business opportunities that are available to us. The following four combinations are possible:

- we can invest in companies
- we can invest in shares
- we can trade companies
- we can trade shares.

Investing in companies

If we are investing in companies, then our perception is that we own part of the company as an asset. The purpose of our assets is to produce passive income, which means that we don't have to work for it. The way that companies produce income for us is by paying an annual dividend, a share of the profits if you like. We may also receive tax credits in the event that the company has already paid some or all of the tax owing on its profits before they are distributed to us, the owners of the company.

The Commonwealth Bank of Australia (ASX code: CBA) is a good example of a public company as an income-producing asset. If you had bought shares in CBA around the time of their initial listing in the second half of 1991, you would have paid approximately $6.50 per share and you would now be receiving an annual dividend payment of approximately $2.60 per share (at the time of writing). That's a very respectable 40 per cent annual return on your original investment. Assets mature over time and CBA, as an income-producing asset, has matured very nicely since its original listing. Let's now examine its recent share price activity by looking at the price chart shown in figure 3.2 (overleaf).

Figure 3.2: Commonwealth Bank share price chart

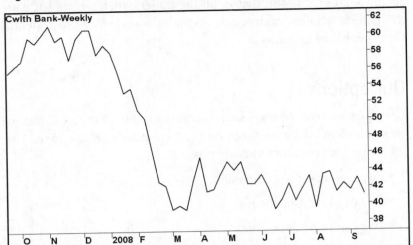

We can see that during this 12-month period, the value of CBA shares has fallen by more than 25 per cent. But, since we own the company as an income-producing asset, the current share price is of little relevance to us. We are only interested in the dividend as a percentage of the price we paid for the shares. The current share price is only important to us if we wish to sell our shares.

If we choose to sell our shares then we will incur capital gains tax (CGT) and lose an income source. That's why it doesn't pay to sell assets. To realise any capital growth on the share price we can borrow against the equity. If you borrow against the equity then you won't have to pay capital gains tax, and if you use the borrowings for further investment purposes then you will even receive a tax deduction on the interest repayments. This is one of the tricks of the wealthy. When the banks lend money against the value of shares, it's called margin lending.

Asset management

Essentially, we want to accumulate assets, not buy and sell them. The teachings of Warren Buffett become extremely relevant when it comes to investing in public companies. I won't go into great detail on how to value public companies but here are several of Buffett's key points:

- you want to own your assets forever; you never want to be forced to sell
- you must very carefully assess the income-producing capabilities of your assets
- you must purchase your assets at the lowest possible price
- your assets must be able to withstand the passage of time
- you should have the attitude that you're buying the actual company itself.

These points apply to property investment as well as investing in public companies. Bearing in mind that Warren Buffett has the financial wherewithal to control the public companies that he buys and we don't, we must be very careful when choosing companies that will last us a lifetime. You can see how this single criterion rules out high technology stocks because of the volatility of their operating environment. This is why Buffett has such a strong preference for companies that produce essential products, such as Coca-Cola, Gillette, and so on.

Investing in either public companies or property could just as easily be called asset management, and good asset managers are anything but passive. Asset management falls under the heading of active investing and we all own assets of some type. This area of active investing is not the focus of this book, but we will revisit the topic in the last chapter when we look at how to identify lifetime income-producing assets.

Investing in shares

This is almost the shortest section in the entire book, and with good reason because:

- the value of our shares reflects the sentiment of the crowd
- shares don't pay dividends, the companies they represent do
- shares are intangible.

Therefore, if you use shares as lifetime assets:

- the value of your assets depends on the sentiment of the crowd at any given moment

- your assets don't produce any income
- you own intangible assets.

While this may appear to be semantics to some, understanding the difference between public companies and shares can be the difference between success and failure in the marketplace. When investing in the stock market it pays to see ourselves as investing in public companies, rather than in the shares themselves.

Trading in companies

This is the shortest section in the entire book. Very few of us have the resources to trade in publicly listed companies. To buy and sell companies for profit obviously requires a huge amount of capital and an even greater amount of skill. Even trying to follow the exponents of this craft is exceptionally difficult. I speak from personal experience, having tried to ride Kerry Packer's coat-tails on more than one occasion.

Trading in shares

This is where things get interesting. We can take full advantage of the intangible nature of shares by trading them for profit. To fully understand what share trading is all about, let's establish some basic definitions.

Shares	→	S-products
Stock market	→	S-store
Information	→	E-products
Online store	→	E-store
Tangible items	→	T-products
Physical store	→	T-store

The world is still trying to come to grips with the advent of the internet and how to exploit it for commercial gain. A few are succeeding at e-commerce but many online entrepreneurs are struggling. A successful e-store has the following obvious advantages:

- no physical infrastructure

- automated transactions
- few staff and/or overheads
- reach (people can visit from anywhere in the world)
- fan-out (thousands of people can visit each day).

But these advantages are only fully exploited if we trade e-products such as:

- money
- shares
- information
- music
- newsletters
- software
- gambling.

In other words, e-products are those that can be transmitted on the internet. T-products are tangible and can't be transmitted on the internet. We still have physical infrastructure, manual processing, staff and higher overheads if we try to sell t-products such as:

- fish
- toys
- furniture
- motorbikes
- groceries
- sporting goods.

While those selling t-products gain the benefit of 'reach' and 'fan-out' if they sell their products online, the back end of their business is still made of bricks and mortar. Many of the successes and failures that have occurred among the Titans of e-commerce confirm the greater viability of only trading e-products in an e-store. The ultimate form of an e-store is an s-store (stock market), because when you trade s-products (shares) you have the added advantages of:

- ready-made customers so there are no advertising costs

- no website costs because your s-store exists only on paper
- products you don't have to manufacture or create
- no delivery or supply problems.

As traders we want to make money by buying and selling shares for profit as efficiently as possible. We only want to hold shares if the price of those shares is going up. We don't want any dead stock sitting on the shelves as it ties up valuable trading capital. Trading shares comes under the auspices of active investing and is the mainstay of this book.

Most people believe that traders are highly active in the marketplace. In fact, how we go about trading shares and how much time we spend doing it depends largely on our objectives. If you're trading shares such as CSL Limited, then all you have to do is glance at a chart (such as the one shown in figure 3.3) each week to make sure the share price is still going up. And since your objective as a trader is to do as little work as possible, shares such as these are well suited to your objectives.

Figure 3.3: CSL share price chart

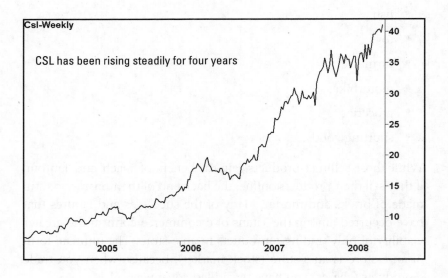

Active investing defined

The definition of active investing is best illustrated by figure 3.4.

Figure 3.4: investors, traders and active investors

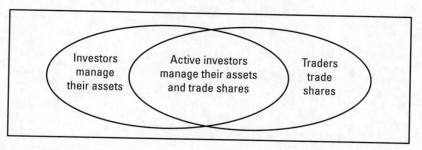

We must be able to differentiate between our income-producing assets and the shares that are our stock-in-trade. Failure to do this is the same folly as trying to sell t-products in an e-store. I have seen portfolios where shares that have crashed in price have been conveniently moved across into the asset column. However, when analysed as income-producing assets they don't stack up, either. The bottom line is that we have to treat these shares like a shopkeeper would treat his dead stock—mark them down and get rid of them.

While s-products can become assets, we must convert them for the right reasons and not due to psychological convenience. As active investors we have many opportunities available to us but in the same manner as all those successful in business, we must manage our assets and our s-store with purpose. If we don't then we'll go the same way as the other 95 per cent of small businesses in Australia, and disappear without a trace.

Chapter 4

The investment business

If it doesn't kill you, it'll make you stronger

Most people who start a small business will sit down and plan how they are going to get started. I speak from personal experience, having owned several small businesses myself. You find a shop, work out what stock and fittings will cost, calculate how long it will take you to start generating an income and then go and see your bank manager, title to the family home in hand.

You start the business after securing a loan against your home and everything goes to plan. After a year or two you're managing to draw a wage and still make some headway on the loan. However, from this point on the business gradually goes from being a lifelong dream to being a millstone around your neck. You are completely at a loss as to how or why you got into this situation in the first place. After all, you planned the whole enterprise so carefully and everything went perfectly to plan. The problem is—you've run out of plan.

For me, it took about 10 years in small business for the penny to finally drop. The whole process began with me admitting that I didn't have all the answers and that I needed help. So I engaged the services of a business coach, Michael. Interestingly, what Michael taught me in business is directly parallel to what I teach other people about the stock market. I've spent years practising certain principles in one area of my life, not realising that the same principles also applied to another.

What many people do is plan to 'start' a business, without planning to 'succeed' in business. Many end up working 50 to 60 hours a week, earning little or no more than the wage they'd walked away from. The worst part is, we become answerable to all of our customers instead of just one boss. Not much of an improvement!

If we don't want to run off the end of our plan then we must set our sights on success and not just on getting started. Our business strategy should be designed to meet our objectives, where the said objectives are geared towards our ultimate success. This is another area of difficulty for many people, as few of us can initially define success. The definition is different for each of us because our goals in life differ.

What is common, though, is that at the end of our working or income-producing lives is retirement. I define retirement as the ability to maintain a lifestyle of my choosing without having to work for it. Where we all differ is in the choice of lifestyle. As individuals we must decide on a lifestyle that we will be happy with and then decide if we have that lifestyle yet, or whether we need to obtain more wealth in order to achieve it.

If you're happy with the house you currently live in, the car you drive, your disposable income, and so on, then all you really want is the ability to stop working for it. You then need to calculate how much income you need each year in order to achieve this. However, if you want a bigger house or a newer car, then you need to increase your wealth — that is, the value of your assets.

If you're in the latter category then you are a candidate for wealth creation, whereas those in the former are only interested in income generation. Mistakenly, many people implement wealth creation strategies by gearing their assets and taking unnecessary risks.

I've spoken to many individuals who've had the wheels fall off a wealth creation strategy unnecessarily. They often lament the fact that they could have retired several years earlier had they not taken risks to achieve wealth they didn't really need in the first place.

Lifestyle freedom

Don't confuse retirement with images of old people sitting around retirement villages. Retirement is just another word for lifestyle freedom. Today, I work because I choose to, and not because I have to generate an income from week to week. I have lifestyle freedom as opposed to mere financial freedom. Financial freedom just means you have the money to do whatever you want.

In a past life I ran a successful IT business for years that gave me the financial freedom to choose where I lived, what make and model of car I drove and where I wanted to go for holidays. The problem was that I had to work 50 to 60 hours every week to maintain this position. Lack of free time imprisoned me. With only financial freedom I rarely wore a smile.

Essentially, the difference between lifestyle freedom and financial freedom is time. So, plan for retirement and not for success. If you're 30 years old, then you'll probably need to consider wealth creation strategies, but if you're in your 40s or 50s then you may simply want to stop working for what you already have. You may even want to adopt a less expensive lifestyle. These are all questions you must answer as individuals, and they need to be answered before you start your business.

The time factor

Once you have quantified your individual objectives then success in business is achieved by meeting those objectives. However, there are other parameters that will affect your business strategy that are only partially under your control. An example of this is the amount of time it will take to achieve success. Attempting to make a million dollars in your first year may be overly ambitious and unrealistic.

Your timeframe will largely be determined by your lifestyle objectives and the extent of your current resources.

A good rule of thumb is to minimise risk by giving yourself as much time as possible and anticipating that your stock market business will return 20 per cent on invested capital per annum. This is my minimum target as anything less makes being in the stock market an inefficient use of my time.

We all begin with varying levels of resources, in terms of both time and money and it's important that we accurately quantify these. I have taught hundreds of people how to trade but few ever actually do it. The primary reason for this is that they try to trade in a way that requires more time than they have to spare. The bottom line is that you will either lose interest in the whole process or lose money if your lifestyle doesn't allow you to meet the demands of your trading strategy.

Many of us are also seduced by the idea that trading is easy because vendors of ready-made trading systems make success look far easier than it actually is. When people realise how much knowledge and effort is required they quickly give up. As an active investor I am prepared to work a maximum of one hour per week, and this requirement will have a large impact on my trading strategy. I don't want to be obliged to check the market every day and I have learnt to allocate my time in business in the same way.

Many small businesses are built around one person's unique skills. If we do this, we are building a prison for ourselves, because we can never step out of the business if we have to work in it to keep it running. A friend of mine who is a school teacher once told me a relevant and amusing story.

When asked what he wanted to be when he grew up, a 10-year-old boy answered that he wanted to be a 'lollipop man' and help school children cross the road. When asked why he replied that he wouldn't have to start working until he was very old. While the solution isn't ideal, his objective is right on the money. But given the shortage of lollipop man vacancies, we will plan to work only one hour per week in our investment business.

To meet this objective you will need to employ the expertise of others. A full-service stockbroker is a handy employee because they can execute your orders during the day and save you the trouble of having to do it yourself using an online broker. Of course, if you're trying to minimise overheads at the start, then an online broker is cheaper. But ultimately you want a full-service stockbroker because they'll save you a lot of time and effort at very little expense.

My stockbroker finetunes my market entries and exits better than I can because he has spent more time doing it and has a better feel for the market. After all, that's his job. When I recommend using a full-service stockbroker most people tell me that they get service which is proportional to the amount of money they have under management. This is absolutely correct, even if stockbrokers deny it, as they are no different from any other service provider in any other industry. If you were a stockbroker you would service your biggest clients first as well.

So do what retailers do. Join forces to give yourself bulk-buying power. I refer all my newsletter subscribers (see back page) to a single stockbroker who I know is highly competent at his job. As a result, he now has millions of dollars under management from my subscribers. When a new subscriber signs up with a capital base of say $30 000, then he or she is treated as part of a much larger pool of funds under management.

He is not argumentative, doesn't undermine his client's strategies and is well aware of what is required of him. If he fails to perform his function to our satisfaction then we will all move our money elsewhere. It's an employer–employee relationship, as it should be if we're running a business and we're the boss.

Prove it then leverage it

If you wish to build wealth then you need to look at how you can gear your existing assets and other methods of leveraging your performance, such as margin lending. Always be aware that any form of leveraging will not only increase your returns but will have the same amplifying effect on your losses. That said, there is a great deal of misunderstanding about borrowing for investment purposes and the inherent risks. We are conditioned in this country to believe that we should only risk money in the stock market that we can afford to lose.

This type of thinking is an overhang from a bygone era where financial security reigned supreme. If you had a roof over your head, food on the table and a shirt on your back, then you didn't do anything to jeopardise the situation. The focus was on job security and everything that fed into it, such as having a good education. On the back of the depression of the 1930s this thinking was highly appropriate but in today's society it is fast becoming obsolete.

The children of today are being prepared for a world that no longer exists.

Today, many highly qualified professionals, who have been gainfully employed all their working lives, now realise they can't depend on the government, their families, or a company pension in retirement. Thirty years ago, all you needed to do was own your home and your retirement income came from one of the aforementioned three sources. You didn't have to take risks in order to maintain your lifestyle. But times change and unfortunately attitudes tend to lag behind the times. Most parents still believe that a good formal education is the single key to financial security. The children of today are being prepared for a world that no longer exists.

Most people in our society sell their time via a full-time job rather than investing their time to make money. Borrowing for personal consumption is also encouraged. If you can maintain an acceptable lifestyle and meet the repayments on your debts, then it's okay to borrow money to improve your lifestyle. This explains why only one per cent of the population is financially self-sufficient.

Most people convert their time to money and then convert their money into depreciating possessions and interest repayments. What's more, the house they live in is not an income-producing asset unless you charge yourself rent. So paying off a mortgage will free up your income while you continue to work, but it will be of little help in generating a retirement income.

While many of us are happy to borrow for personal consumption, most people believe that you should only invest money in the stock market that you are prepared to lose. In fact, you can't lose all of your money in the stock market unless every share you owned delisted. As active investors we are going to trade only in blue-chip stocks and, using recent history as a guide, the worst case scenario is a 50 per cent loss during a stock market crash. So you can actually use *twice* the amount of money in the stock market that you're prepared to lose.

The tax office will also allow you to claim interest repayments on capital borrowed for investment purposes as a tax deduction. Let's look at using leverage in a sensible way by going back to a simple small business scenario. We'll assume you're buying and selling widgets from home, and that:

- you buy widgets for $10 and sell them for $13
- you place an advertisement in a local newspaper for $50
- you sell 20 widgets as a result, giving you a gross profit of $60
- after you pay for the advertisement you have a net profit of $10.

Your $50 advertisement has yielded a 20 per cent return. Having tested and measured the sales from your advertisement and documented the whole process, you are now ready to leverage your little part-time business, so:

- using the aforementioned documentation you *prove* to the bank that your enterprise is profitable
- you borrow $1000 and place five $200 advertisements
- your gross profit each week is now $1200 given a yield of 20 per cent on all advertising.
- after you pay for your advertisements you have a net profit of $200 per week
- you repay the loan and get someone else to run your business for $50 per week
- by just monitoring the business you are now making $150 per week.

This is a simple example of how gearing can be used to 'grow' a business strategy that has first been proven on a small scale. Compare this approach with someone who leaves their job, borrows against the family home and starts a nursery. If you ask why they're prepared to risk the family home on a business venture, they will probably cite the fact that if another nursery down the road can succeed, then so can they. Now there are two guys working 50 to 60 hours per week running nurseries.

In the stock market you can use gearing to grow your business once you have established that it's profitable and minimised the risk. Only then can you consider using home equity or margin lending for leverage. Unlike most other businesses, in the stock market you can even have a practice run, commonly referred to as paper trading, honing your skills before risking any real money.

Market psychology

Once we've established our objectives and planned for success we must examine one of the most difficult aspects of trading or investing in the stock market—psychology. Newcomers to the market will probably consider the remainder of this chapter as either trivial or irrelevant. I can assure you from personal experience that its relevance will increase with the time you spend in the marketplace. The most important reason for having clear objectives and an unambiguous market strategy is that our greatest problem is us. Our own emotions and instincts work very hard at undermining our strategy.

Following the herd

A good place to start examining the psychology of trading is stock market crashes. Imagine that you've just come home from work and as you pull into the drive you notice that your neighbour has bought himself a new car. It has no great impact on you other than that you wonder how someone in their position could afford it. Once inside, your partner tells you that their sister is going overseas with money that she made from the stock market.

After you've eaten dinner, you stroll down the road to the front of Peter's house. He's a neighbour who meets you on weeknights for an evening walk. Peter tells you that there won't be too many more of these walks because he can now afford to move to a bigger and better house thanks to his share portfolio. You look at him, slightly worried now, and tell him that you suspect your neighbour must be in shares or something similar, because he's just bought a new car. Peter laughs and tells you that he gave your neighbour a tip some time ago on some hot resource stocks. You both agree that this was probably the source of your neighbour's new-found wealth. But while you smile and joke about not getting the tip yourself, you're beginning to feel genuinely anxious.

Knowledge is not the same as doing ...

Later that evening, your partner raises the issue of buying some shares, because just about all of their friends are doing it and making money. Greed is not going through your mind, but the terrible thought of being left behind as your entire social circle moves up the socioeconomic scale without you. Anxiety and fear drive you into buying shares and joining in the frenzy because your fear of being left behind overrides the thought of losing money.

As you can see, the crowd mentality that drives stock markets up has little to do with greed and much to do with our desire to stay with the pack. Fear of separation will keep herds of animals together as they stampede off a cliff and the effect on human beings is much the same. The idea that crashes are precipitated purely by greed is a fallacy put forth by the 'I told you so' crowd, who are so afraid of being wrong they never participate in anything. This crowd consists largely of highly knowledgeable people who avoid potential failure by never taking part themselves.

Knowledge won't protect against losses

Knowledge will not protect you from losses if you're going to participate in the stock market. Knowing is not the same as doing in many human endeavours and investing is one of them. Imagine if a surgeon was going to operate on you but told you that they'd never performed an operation before in their life. Would you feel any better if they told you that they had been studying for 20 years and there wasn't anything they didn't know when it came to this particular procedure?

We feel comfortable about a subject if we're highly knowledgeable about it. This is why many people start out in the stock market by acquiring all the knowledge they can. I have met people who know far more about the stock market than I do, but have never bought a single share. They have invested too much time and money learning about the stock market to take a chance on suffering a loss and being, as they perceive it, wrong. Similarly, people will not sell and cut their losses because to do so would be to admit that they were wrong in buying the shares in the first place. These people put the shares in the bottom drawer and become passive share investors in order to protect their self-esteem.

Self-righteousness

As well as finding comfort in being right, we also feel protected by it. Some years ago while driving to my doctor's surgery, I turned left at a large intersection. However, I failed to look for drivers doing a right-hand turn into the same road. At the last minute, I saw that I was on a collision course with just such a vehicle and slammed on the brakes. As I was travelling at 70 kilometres per hour, it was a fairly dramatic situation.

It suddenly dawned on me that the other driver hadn't taken any evasive action. Had we collided, I would have hit his car with enough impact to kill anyone sitting on the left-hand side of the car. As I came to a halt, just inches away, I looked at the other driver to see him looking back at me with a smug expression on his face. Usually when I'm about to kill someone through incompetence they are inclined towards being angry with me rather than feeling smug. I strongly suspect the other driver didn't take any evasive action because he was technically in the right. He came very close to being dead right.

Children... make excellent share traders.

Have you ever heard the expression, 'The price of this share *should* go up'? With this thinking, many people will lose money on shares as long as they can be self-righteous in doing so. Inevitably, these people will leave the marketplace with resentment towards those of us who remain in it, because they see us as being collectively wrong and acting irrationally and irresponsibly with our money.

Status

As adults, we live in a world where social status is often judged by how much money we have and how knowledgeable we are. Judging people on these values comes from our social conditioning, and our self-esteem becomes dependent on these same values. Children, on the other hand, don't use the same yardsticks as adults and, for this reason, they make excellent share traders.

Every time a teacher undertakes a pretend share trading project with a class of children, the results are invariably successful. This is because children latch on to a trading strategy and are not thwarted by their own psychology. They don't become emotionally attached to their choices, nor are they ashamed of the losses they will incur if they sell out of a losing position.

Greed

Greed also plays a part in the stock market and has cost me thousands of dollars over the years. For example, say you enter the marketplace with a plan to achieve an annual return of between 20 per cent and 50 per cent per annum. You have shares in your portfolio that have gone up by 20 per cent in a single month. These shares are showing an annual rate of return of 240 per cent, which is six times greater than your original objective of 20 per cent to 50 per cent. The rational thing to do would be to take the money and run, but greed kicks in and the internal wealth calculator goes to work.

Your thinking is that if you compounded 20 per cent per month, then you would achieve an annual return of 892 per cent. Multiply that by the original purchase of $3000 worth of shares, and you have a profit of $23760. Then you start spending the profits and before you know it, you *need* the shares to keep going up at this rate. We hope surgeons don't become distracted thinking about how they're going to spend the fee they're going to make on an operation while they're actually performing it.

Because we are dealing directly with money in the stock market, our greed can surface very easily. It blinds us to the task at hand. Most people only become aware of their greed when they begin to trade, which makes share trading a very revealing process.

Role play

In any type of small business the owners undertake several roles. In my business I am the CEO, the sales manager, the administrator and even the cleaner. I am constantly switching hats as I move from one task to the next. In a lot of small businesses, the owner will focus on a favourite activity and neglect other areas which are just as vital to success. We face the same difficulty in the active investing business, as we have to set the objectives, design the strategy and execute it.

It's very easy to become overly focused on the role of strategist, to forget or change our original objectives to suit the strategy, and to try to tweak the strategy as we are executing it. As a result, we lose focus and fall victim to our emotions as they override our original purpose. Many investors and traders are unable to assess their basic market strategy accurately because they have never executed it fully and precisely.

We must separate the three functions of CEO, strategist and trader. One way we can do this is to role play. Let's play a game called, 'Monkeys in space'. We can use this simple game to separate the three functions and override our emotions as required. The three roles are:

- the US Government (CEO)
- NASA chief engineer (strategist)
- the monkey that orbits the earth (trader).

The success of this game has absolutely nothing to do with making money, so we should be able to overcome our greed. The purpose of the game is to put a monkey in space, have it orbit the earth and then return safely, which parallels buying, holding and selling a share. I'll go through each role separately and identify its function, as well as suggest who may undertake the role other than ourselves.

The US Government

The US Government is you or yourself and your partner. The government's job is to set the ultimate goals for the NASA space program. In other words, it's your job to determine the ultimate objectives of your investment business. You will need to consult the chief engineer at NASA to ensure that your objectives are realistic and achievable if the space program is to be successful for the next few years.

Once you have established the objectives of the space program (your investment objectives) you will hand them on to the chief engineer. It is the chief engineer's job to establish and implement a program that will meet those objectives in the time specified. The chief engineer must also report back to you regularly with progress reports. You must monitor their performance to ensure that the program is on target to meet your objectives because if it doesn't, you won't be re-elected.

As the government, you want to monitor the space program constantly to make sure that the chief engineer doesn't get carried away and take unnecessary risks. You definitely don't want one of your space capsules to crash down in a populated area because some rocket scientist at NASA started fast-tracking the program. To meet your responsibilities you have control over the funding for the space program and you also have the authority to dismiss any of the staff at NASA if you deem it necessary (that is, your partner may want to replace you as chief engineer).

It's also up to the government to insist that NASA proves the feasibility of any program it wants funding for. You decide the question of risk in your investment business, whether gearing is appropriate and/ or the amount of starting capital. It is perfectly reasonable for you to decide on paper trading until there are proven results before undertaking any level of risk. This role is best undertaken by both partners. Governments that are run by presidents not answerable to a Congress have a tendency to be a little too lax with their expectations, particularly if they're also playing the role of chief engineer.

NASA's chief engineer

The chief engineer's job is to develop and implement a space program that will meet the objectives set down by the government. They will be consulted by the government when it sets these objectives, and must ensure that they are achievable and realistic. The chief engineer also decides whether further research and development is necessary prior to undertaking space missions.

In other words, as the strategist it is your responsibility to ensure that you have the ability, the appropriate knowledge, and the necessary tools to implement your chosen market strategy. Tragically, many chief engineers have a nasty habit of turning into mad scientists driven by their emotions and personal ambitions. For this reason, we must ensure that our chief engineer is answerable to others and that they don't try to fly their own missions. That's the monkey's job.

The monkey

Preferably, the monkey will be played by a partner rather than the same person playing the engineer. Failing this, the monkey's role should be played by both partners to ensure that mission orders are adhered to. We don't want to implement a market strategy only to have it altered midway by our own greed, fear or anxiety.

The monkey has what appears to be the easiest job of all. It must follow the instructions set out by the chief engineer to the letter and not use any personal discretion in implementing them. In other words, if the green light comes on then the monkey presses the green button, and so forth. If the monkey has to exercise discretion to make the strategy work then the engineer hasn't done their job properly and the strategy needs to be altered.

You must have a complete strategy that includes stock selection, when to buy and when to sell. Too often people will choose a stock, buy the shares, and then rely on their personal discretion the rest of the way. While the monkey's job sounds like an easy one, it is the one role where your emotions and anxieties will be trying to take over. If the monkey does its job well, regardless of whether we see profits or losses at the end of the day, the chief engineer will have solid data from completed missions to help adjust and improve the strategy.

Make changes to your market strategy away from the market, and not when you are in the middle of executing your trades. Putting the whole process in chronological order, you should:

- set your objectives
- develop your strategy and only acquire knowledge which is relevant
- implement your strategy with total discipline
- adjust your strategy as results dictate
- periodically review your advancement toward your objectives.

The company we keep

The final area we need to look at is the effect that others can have on our attitudes. Our personal psychology and attitude can be derailed by those around us, as well as by ourselves. If outside influences undermine us we must isolate ourselves from them. People who underachieve will instinctively try to bring those around them down to the same level because it will make them feel better about themselves. For this reason, many traders refrain from discussing their trades with others. Obviously, this will eliminate any unwanted criticism.

Negative people hang around with negative people. Successful people hang around golf clubs and beach resorts. We need to focus on ourselves and work at improving our own performance, just like successful athletes. World-class golfers worry about their own score card and champion swimmers focus on beating their personal best times. Likewise, self-understanding and self-management are very much the keys to success in the stock market.

Chapter 5

Fools, facts and factions

Seek profits, not perfection

Once we've set our objectives, we must develop an understanding of the stock market itself and the forces that move share prices. Share price movements are the result of many variables working together to give what appears to be a random outcome. But true randomisation occurs only where there is a complete absence of organisation. Therefore, while share price movements approximate randomisation, they are not truly random. The big question is whether we can find, and exploit, patterns in share price movements to create profits.

If we are successful, then we should beat the performance of the All Ordinaries index every time. As it would be impossible to examine *all* of the variables that influence the market, we will look only at the major factors that affect the crowd's behaviour. Some of these have little to do with logic, but if they influence all or part of the crowd then they are worthy of examination. The stock market is a capitalist democracy where one dollar equals one vote, be it a fool's dollar or otherwise.

Fundamental analysis

Fundamental analysis, or financial analysis, is the oldest and largest school of thought when it comes to evaluating the price of shares. Fundamentalists place a value on a public company based on its underlying financials, and then value shares in the company by inference. A fundamentalist will decide whether a share price is too high or too low and act accordingly. If the crowd is undervaluing a company and its performance by pricing its shares below fair value, then the fundamentalist would buy the shares. Alternatively, if a fundamentalist owns shares that are priced a long way above their fair value, then they would sell the shares.

Ben Graham is ... the father of financial analysis ...

Ben Graham is widely considered to be the father of financial analysis and his teachings have spawned modern giants of the investment industry such as Warren Buffett. Graham's philosophy for success is centred on the following benchmarks:

- Profitable enterprises should be based on factual information, not optimism.

- A portfolio should contain a minimum of 10 to a maximum of 30 holdings.

- Companies should be financially large; that is, they should have high market capitalisation or be blue chip.

- Companies should be managed in a financially conservative manner; that is, with low debt.

- Companies should have an unbroken history of paying dividends for the past 20 years.

- The ratio of the company's market value to its earnings (P/E ratio) should not exceed 25.

- The company's market value should not be greater than 1.5 times its net tangible assets.

Ben Graham bought or held companies which met these criteria and sold when the companies ceased to do so, either because of a rising share price or changes in the company's financial position. However, the benchmarks used by Ben Graham, while well suited to investing in stocks nearly 100 years ago, are not necessarily optimal for modern times. Today, financial analysis is so widely used and accepted that service providers such as stockbrokers and funds managers can legally justify the advice they give clients on this basis alone.

Fundamental analysis centres on the financial performance of public companies and is the mainstay of both individual and institutional investment strategies. If it were the only factor used by the crowd then shares would always track the value of the underlying companies. Modern fundamentalists use an ever-increasing range of techniques to assess the financial status of public companies. Some of the more widely used are worth examining.

Market capitalisation

Virtually all of the techniques used by fundamentalists employ the market capitalisation of a company. The market capitalisation is the current share price of a company multiplied by the number of shares issued. Therefore, a company whose share price is $10 and which has one million shares on issue would have a market capitalisation of $10 million. The market capitalisation, among other things, can then be used to compare the share price to the earnings and asset backing of the company.

Price/earnings ratio

'Price/earnings ratio', or 'P/E Ratio', defines the relationship between a company's market capitalisation and its annual net earnings after tax. For example:

- a company has a total market capitalisation of $10 million
- its annual net earnings after tax are $1 million
- therefore, it has a P/E ratio of 10 ($10 million ÷ $1 million).

Investors look for lower P/E ratios when buying shares and will sell shares in companies with higher P/E ratios. The P/E ratio must be recalculated whenever the share price of a company changes or a new financial report is issued.

Price/asset ratio

'Price/asset ratio', or 'P/A ratio', defines the relationship between a company's market capitalisation and its net tangible assets. To demonstrate:

- a company has a total market capitalisation of $10 million
- its total net tangible assets, that is, property, plant, equipment, and so on, are $2.5 million
- therefore, it has a P/A ratio of 4 ($10 million ÷ $2.5 million).

Investors prefer a low P/A ratio. It is possible to find companies with P/A ratios of less than one, which means that a $1 share represents more than $1 of value in net tangible assets. This situation occurs when the future prospects of a company are poor and the marketplace is more focused on earnings than on asset backing. To avoid this situation, fundamentalists look for companies with both a low P/E ratio, indicating good earnings, and a low P/A ratio. In doing this, many fundamentalists believe they have discovered a truly undervalued share.

Dividend yield

Investors who place a greater emphasis on income as opposed to capital growth are always very interested in the dividend yield. Dividend yield stands for the percentage of a company's share price that is paid to an investor annually in the form of dividends. The dividend yield is expressed as a percentage and is often compared with bank interest rates. So, if a share is trading at $10 and the company pays an annual dividend of 50 cents, the current dividend yield would be five per cent.

The earning capacity of a company is reflected through its ability to pay a good dividend as well as its P/E ratio. Assuming that dividend yields track interest rates, and the price of your shares goes up, then the annual dividend payment should rise. So over time your initial investment will mature and you can monitor this growth by calculating the dividend yield using your original purchase price, as follows:

- You bought the shares at $10 each and the dividend yield was five per cent (dividend of 50¢).

- The share price has risen over time to $20 and the dividend yield is still five per cent.

- Therefore, the *current* dividend payment is now $1 per share ($1 \div 20 \times 100 = 5\%$).

- The dividend yield, using your original purchase price, is 10 per cent ($1 per $10 share).

A modern derivative of these financial yardsticks is to study the change in a company's financial performance over time. This can be done in a variety of ways. For instance, we might compare the earnings of the current financial year with those of the previous year to see if there is any improvement. If a company's earnings have increased from $1 million to $1.2 million over the course of one year, then it's said that the company has achieved earnings growth of 20 per cent.

We can also look at the quality of the management of the company by comparing gross and net earnings from one year to the next. If a company has achieved gross earnings of $5 million for two years running but has reported net earnings in the second year higher than that of the first, then we can infer that the financial management of the company has improved. They have managed to reduce either their overheads or their tax liability, or both. Fundamental analysis, being the mainstay of private and institutional investing, has a major influence on share price movements.

Technical analysis

Technical analysis, or charting, is the study of price activity itself. Chartists, using either pattern recognition or mathematical indicators, observe and infer future price movements from historical price activity. Charting purists believe that all the factors which affect price movements are present in price charts and that these factors can be studied without having to look beyond the charts themselves.

The weekly bar chart (shown in figure 5.1, overleaf) shows just over six months of price activity. The vertical scale is the share price in dollars and the horizontal scale is time. Note that there are approximately four bars to each month, with each bar representing five days because shares are not traded over the course of the weekend.

Figure 5.1: weekly bar chart

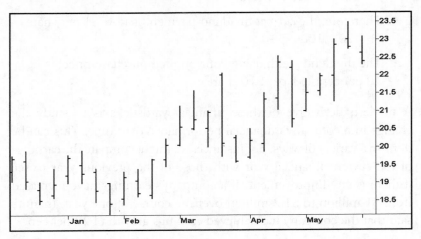

In the above chart, each week is represented by a bar, which has a tick on the left and another tick on the right. The top of the bar and the bottom of the bar represent the price range of trading for the week, that is, the highest and the lowest price. The tick to the left of the bar is the opening price of the week and the tick to the right represents the closing price for the week. The share price is currently trending upwards and a trend trader who uses technical analysis will buy into this market for this reason alone. Trend traders have no interest in why the crowd is buying up the share price, only in the fact that it is going up during the time the shares are held.

Charting has been used for centuries to analyse price movements in a variety of markets. Before the age of computers, charts would be drawn using graph paper, pencil and ruler. Although technical analysis has existed for as long as financial markets have, it has only come into wide use in the past several decades, thanks to the advent of computer-aided drawing and personal computers.

However, the majority of individual investors still do not use charting at all, while institutional investors who have adopted it continue to give greater importance to fundamental analysis. Charting is often seen as the mainstay of short-term traders only, and is sometimes unfairly equated with crystal ball gazing and fortune telling as a means of making investment decisions.

A modern extension of charting is the use of technical indicators to provide mechanical buy and sell signals, thus alleviating the chartist's reliance on discretion. A simple method of using technical indicators to trade shares is by applying a nine-day and a 21-day simple moving average (SMA) to a daily price chart. A simple moving average is created in the following way:

- Calculate the average closing price over a given number of days and plot it on a price chart as a dot on the current day.
- As each day occurs, recalculate the average price and plot a new dot on that day.
- Draw an unbroken line connecting the dots of each day.

A nine-day SMA is calculated using the closing price from the previous nine days, while a 21-day SMA uses the closing price from the previous 21 days. The nine-day moving average tracks the current price activity more closely than the 21-day moving average. When the nine-day SMA (grey line) crosses above the 21-day SMA (black line), then a buy signal is generated. When the nine-day SMA crosses *below* the 21-day SMA, then a sell signal is generated. This technique is shown in figure 5.2.

Figure 5.2: buy and sell signals

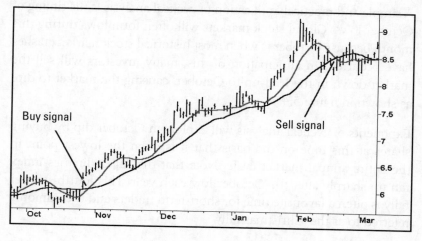

This simple method is a trend-following technique and prevents us from buying or holding shares that are falling in price. See figure 5.3 for an example.

Figure 5.3: the benefit of sell signals

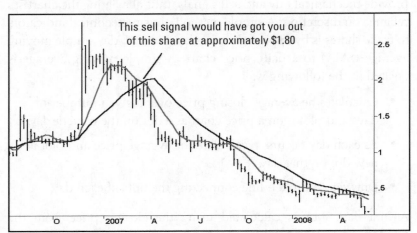

Cyclical analysis

Cyclical analysis, as the name implies, is the study of market cycles. This form of analysis is another extension of technical analysis. Patterns can occur over time that are predictable and those chartists who use cyclical analysis will attempt to predict price movements on the assumption that these patterns will be repetitious.

A simple and practical application of cyclical analysis is the timing of October lows. Global stock markets will often form lows during this month because October is when most historical stock market crashes have occurred. In anticipation of this, many investors will sell the market down in the lead-up to October, causing the market to dip, as shown in figure 5.4.

Exponents of cyclical analysis will exploit an October dip by buying shares at this time on the basis that it is often the lowest point in the entire annual market cycle. Note that the All Ordinaries index ran up sharply after the October low each year. This fourth-quarter rally is often a favourite time for short-term traders and is commonly referred to as the 'Christmas rally'.

Figure 5.4: October lows

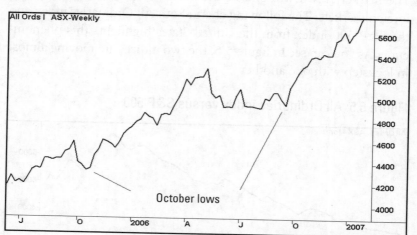

October lows

Factors that affect opinion

Aside from fundamentals, there are several other major factors that have an influence on crowd opinion, and therefore crowd behaviour. Following is a brief summary on each. Further explanation of the effects of these factors on the active investing strategy is given in chapter 11.

Global factors

The US financial markets represent approximately 50 per cent of world stock markets in terms of market capitalisation. To clarify, the market capitalisation of Microsoft Corporation alone is greater than that of the entire South Korean stock market. The Australian stock market, on the other hand, represents only about one per cent of world financial markets and is often said to be the tail, while the United States is the dog. We follow the lead of the US market and to a lesser extent, the Asian markets, which we are considered a part of.

Asian markets have an influence because our resources sector, which has long been considered the mainstay of our stock market, sells the bulk of its output to manufacturers in Asian countries. As a result of this, the behaviour of these foreign markets also has a strong impact on share prices in Australia.

The market crowd will often react blindly to any changes in these foreign markets. The following chart of our All Ordinaries index and the S&P 500 index from the United States highlights this phenomenon. As you can see in figure 5.5, the two indices are moving almost in lockstep with one another.

Figure 5.5: All Ordinaries index versus S&P 500

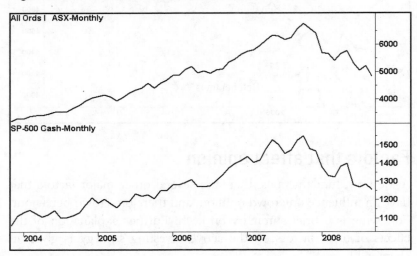

It should also be noted that the effect of foreign markets on the Australian stock market is greatly exacerbated by the fact that our funds managers follow their offshore counterparts. These funds managers control large blocks of capital and therefore have a powerful influence over share price movements.

To summarise, if the US banking sector moves downwards overnight, then our banking sector will likely follow. Furthermore, our markets are open to foreign institutional investors and if they're feeling bullish or bearish on a particular sector, then this sentiment will be reflected across all the markets they are exposed to.

Macro economics

Within financial circles there is often debate over who is really the most powerful man in America. Is it the President of the United States, or Ben Bernanke, Chairman of the United States Federal Reserve?

The Federal Reserve controls official interest rates in the US and can indirectly influence world stock markets. Ben Bernanke, being the Chairman, can move world financial markets just by uttering a few words on what he perceives to be the state of the United States economy.

The effect of macro economics on the market crowd is complex and most economists struggle to understand it. The most predictable link between macro economics and share prices is the very lever which Ben Bernanke controls — interest rates. If interest rates go up, then share prices generally go down because dividend yields generally track official interest rates. The opposite is also true. Falling interest rates will inevitably cause share prices to rise.

News and events

Unpredictable events that occur around the world can have a massive impact on the crowd and how they behave in the marketplace. A classic example of this is the effect that the terrorist attacks in the US on September 11, 2001 had on all world equity markets, including ours, as shown in figure 5.6 (overleaf).

The events of September 11 played a very influential role in causing our market to temporarily dip over 10 per cent. News and world events such as this have a powerful and unpredictable influence on the sentiment of the crowd and correspondingly on share prices. The difficulty in these situations is deciding whether or not the impact is going to be temporary and, therefore, what is the most appropriate course of action.

Gambling and speculation

Any member of the market crowd with money to buy and sell shares has some degree of control over share prices. Speculators, and even those who gamble in the stock market, have influence. This influence is generally unpredictable, short-term and is felt more acutely among smaller capitalisation stocks than blue-chip stocks. Speculators' actions are largely dictated by tips, rumours, media articles, and so on, and they are often easily influenced by the broader market crowd.

Figure 5.6: All Ordinaries index slump after September 11

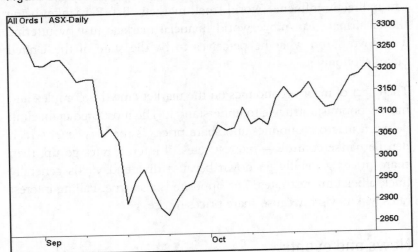

Analysts and gurus

Many members of the crowd will also follow the opinions, teachings and predictions of market gurus. What's more, gurus are virtually impossible to avoid. Many popular market commentators who write for newspapers and magazines will become gurus of sorts without even intending to do so. This is due to our desire to be led, rather than to have to think for ourselves. It also gives us the escape hatch of blame, should something go wrong.

I have known several investors who, over a long period of time, have based all their investment decisions on the opinions and advice of others. Over the years they have moved their focus from one market analyst or guru, to another. As soon as one falls off their pedestal, they appoint another who, sooner or later, suffers the same fate.

As a result of guru-worshipping, the opinions of market analysts, commentators and experts influence the crowd and move share prices. Some years ago, I personally suffered at the hands of a US market analyst who brought out an unfavourable report on News Corporation. The effect of this report is shown in figure 5.7.

I was using derivatives to trade News Corporation during, what I anticipated to be, the fourth-quarter rally following a significant

October low. Everything was going exactly to plan until the analyst, who had been very fond of News Corporation, suddenly brought out a report which downgraded the stock by nearly 30 per cent. His reasons for doing so were based on the belief that News Corporation's recent efforts at setting up a spin-off company that would concentrate on satellite communications were doomed to failure. The downgrading of News Corp's market value was therefore justified given this reduction in future prospects.

Figure 5.7: News Corp share price following an adverse report

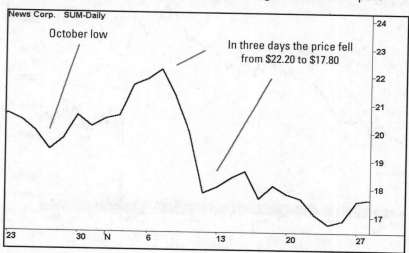

As the US markets trade overnight, I woke up the next morning to find this analyst's report plastered all over the internet and CNBC. The net result was a fall in the price of News Corporation's shares by nearly 20 per cent over the next three days. This analyst's reversal of attitude wiped billions off the company's market value. Debating whether the analyst was right or wrong won't change the effect it had on the crowd and the resulting impact it had on the share price of News Corporation.

Crowd behaviour

The best way of showing the effect of crowd or herd behaviour on stock markets is with charts. The following chart (figure 5.8, overleaf) of the Dow Jones index covering the 1987 stock market crash shows how the US market ran up from 1900 to a peak of 2700 over eight months, an increase of over 40 per cent, and then fell all the way back again in a matter of days. Note the spike in the volume histogram (at the bottom of figure 5.8), which shows the total number of shares traded during the panic selling that took place in late October, a classic indication of a major crash.

Figure 5.8: the 1987 stock market crash

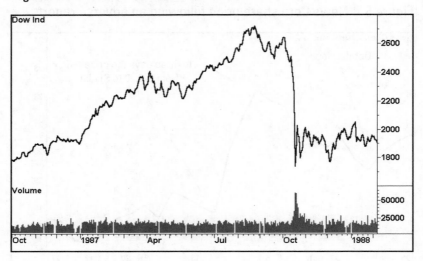

From October 1999 to March 2000 the NASDAQ climbed from 2600 to a peak of 5000. The index virtually doubled in the space of only five months. The subsequent correction in April 2000, shown in figure 5.9, is hardly surprising in hindsight. The crowd was behaving like a herd and logic was replaced with anxiety, fear and greed that was to collectively wipe billions off the value of this market.

Further evidence of crowd behaviour is the market correction of 2007–08, which involved all global equity markets. It is probably the first time in the history of financial markets that we have seen a 'global crowd' act in unison to push down equity markets across the world as if they were a single entity. This phenomenon has been largely aided by the growing efficiency of global communications, which investors have enthusiastically embraced.

Figure 5.9: the NASDAQ correction of April 2000

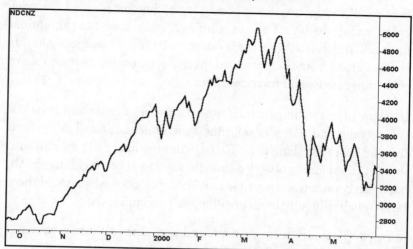

There is no single solution

Over the years, factions have formed around different types of analysis and trading techniques. Fundamentalists typically believe in analysing markets from a purely factual perspective, while many speculators trust their feel for the mood of the marketplace. There are countless books and mountains of information available on a massive range of individual investment techniques and forms of analysis. This information is the quicksand that most of us end up sinking into on our early forays into the marketplace. A typical reaction to this dilemma is to camp on a single technique, which becomes our one and only truth.

Camping on a single truth is a short cut, which we all use, to cope with the pressures of busy modern life. If we can intellectually justify it, then we become inseparable from it. Go for a walk around your neighbourhood and look at the cars in the driveways. Members of the same family will take the easy option of buying the same make, and often model, of car as other members of their family. The logic is that if a particular make of car is reliable and meets the needs of one family member, there is no need to look further for another.

While our motoring needs can be satisfied this way, it is a bad philosophy when it comes to the stock market. Disciples of one investment technique will often denounce other market strategies because of the apparently opposing logic. Fundamentalists consider chart reading to be a form of astrology, while chartists use annual financial reports to line the bottoms of their birdcages. All this conflict arises from the perceived inverse relationship between share price movements and financial ratios.

If a share price is falling then sentiment must be negative and a chartist will recommend that you sell. But a fundamentalist will advise you that the lower the share price is, the better the financial ratios are and that it is therefore probably a time to buy. But if both techniques are based on common sense and sound concepts, then why should there be so much difficulty in reconciling the two approaches?

Most people adopt a single truth and denounce all others to avoid tackling this dilemma. Unfortunately, just being able to justify one's thinking has little to do with making money, particularly in the stock market. Logic doesn't move share prices, opinions do.

There are many instances where share price movements have defied logic. The following chart from the start of the new millennium shows what happened to Telstra Corporation's share price when it announced an Australian corporate record profit of $2.4 billion. The market was disappointed with the announcement for reasons other than the profit itself. As a result, the record profit caused little more than a hiccup in the downward slide of Telstra's share price, as shown in figure 5.10.

In a similar vein, when Billiton Limited (BHP) announced a record loss of over $2 billion in April 1999, it had no noticeable negative impact on the share price. People were more interested in the appointment of a new CEO and the Asian recovery that was beginning to drive up commodity prices at the time. This is illustrated in figure 5.11.

If there are no absolutes in the marketplace then it also follows that there is no single, perfect technique for buying and selling shares. Using the nine-day and 21-day moving average crossover methods to trade the uptrend in News Corporation, as shown in figure 5.12 (on page 76), would have resulted in a loss of profits because of a false sell signal or, as chartists would say, a 'whipsaw'.

Figure 5.10: Telstra share price in relation to profit report

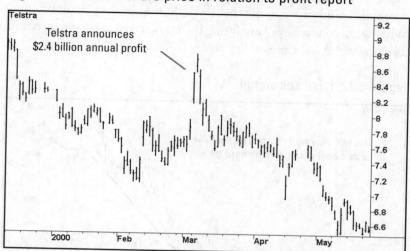

Telstra announces
$2.4 billion annual profit

Figure 5.11: BHP share price in relation to profit report

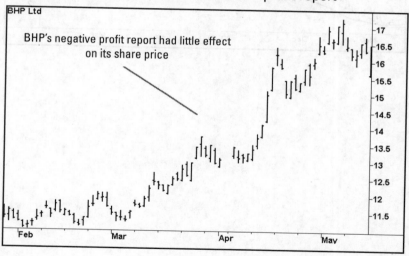

BHP's negative profit report had little effect
on its share price

These examples illustrate the folly of relying on facts or pursuing perfection with a single technique. The reality is that the marketplace is a melting pot of many truths, techniques, strategies, attitudes and emotions. What's more, we cannot achieve perfection when attempting to untangle and track every single variable affecting share price movements. The best that we can hope for is to put the balance of probability in our favour and, indeed, that is all we have to do in order to achieve profits. Personally, I would use tea-leaf reading if someone could prove to me that it would improve my bank balance. What we need is a way of analysing the market that takes into account as many variables as possible.

Figure 5.12: false sell signal

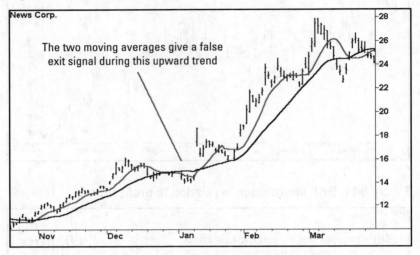

Chapter 6

Introducing dynamic analysis

Bad advice: 'Buy low, sell high'

The simple dynamic that drives share prices either up or down is shown in figure 6.1. Note the use of the word 'factors' as opposed to the word 'facts' in the first square.

Figure 6.1: the driving force of share prices

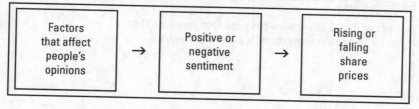

This diagram summarises the whole process that moves share prices up and down and is the foundation of dynamic analysis. We can take most of the elements described in the previous chapter and place them into the square on the left hand side of the diagram. Fundamentals, market cycles, macroeconomics, and so forth, are all factors that affect people's opinion. So, investors who rely on fundamentals are coming at the market dynamic from the left-hand side. Chartists, on the other hand, are coming at the market from the opposite direction by simply measuring the output of the whole process.

As active investors, we will approach the market dynamic from *both ends* by employing dynamic analysis. We will search for blue-chip stocks with both good fundamentals, *and* rising share prices. We can locate such stocks by testing and measuring the entire market dynamic. The following charts (figures 6.2, 6.3 and 6.4) show the results we can achieve by using this process.

Figure 6.2: CSL share price chart

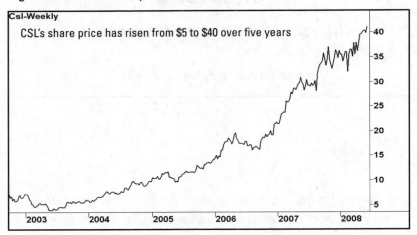

Figure 6.3: Incitec Pivot share price chart

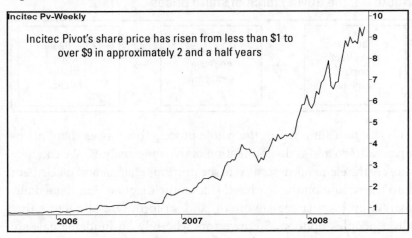

Figure 6.4: Invocare share price chart

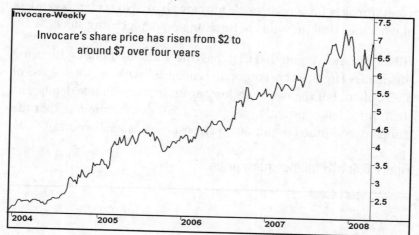

These are the types of shares we want to own because we only make money when the share price is rising. While we should constantly monitor the financial facts relating to our lifetime assets, in the stock market we buy and sell share prices, not fundamentals. This testing and measuring of blue-chip stocks with good fundamentals leads us to reject the shares in the following examples.

Telstra is the number-one stock owned by Australians and its share price has been in gradual decline almost since it first listed on the ASX in the late 1990s (see figure 6.5).

Figure 6.5: Telstra falling share price

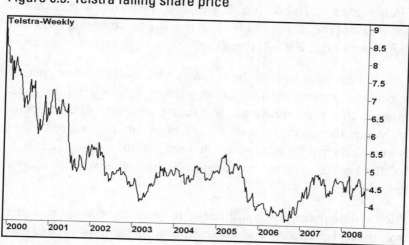

While it may be considered by some a good lifetime income-producing asset, it makes for a poor stock-in-trade share. No trader, regardless of what they deal in, wants to be sitting on depreciating stock.

HIH Insurance Limited (HIH) has the dubious honour of being Australia's largest-ever corporate collapse, with a total loss of $5.3 billion. For the two years leading up to its inevitable demise, its share price fell constantly (see figure 6.6), despite the fact that the company continued to put out very positive financial reports.

Figure 6.6: HIH falling share price

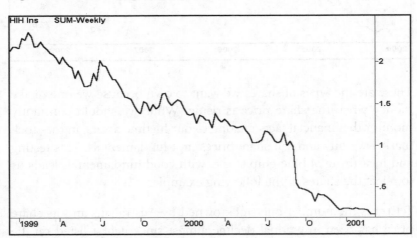

Both of these companies were initially considered to have reasonable fundamentals and good future prospects. However, when we test and measure the share price we find that it was falling and therefore market sentiment towards these shares was, by inference, negative.

Let's digress and look at how fundamentalists view the market dynamic. Conventional investment wisdom ignores sentiment and assumes that if the financials and future prospects of a company are good, then positive market sentiment can be assumed. This is absolutely true, given sufficient time, as shown in figure 6.7. So, the age-old reliance on patience is invaluable when it comes to investing.

I do exercise patience when it comes to my lifetime assets reaching maturity and generating a positive cash flow, but there's no need to wait when buying and selling shares for profit. By testing and measuring the market dynamic as an active investor, you can eliminate the time factor (see figure 6.8).

Figure 6.7: conventional investment wisdom

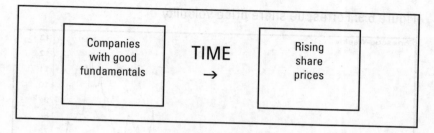

Figure 6.8: investment wisdom for active investors

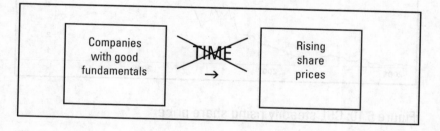

But if you ignore good fundamentals and just look for rising share prices, then be prepared for some nasty surprises. Take the case of Fortescue Metals Group Ltd (figure 6.9, overleaf), an iron-ore producer, which has seen its market capitalisation up in the billions of dollars despite the fact that it didn't post any earnings until early 2008.

Given that its share price has been driven more by market sentiment than its underlying fundamentals, Fortescue has always been characterised by high volatility and is capable of falling at a rapid rate. This makes it a stock that requires close and constant attention.

Dynamic analysis employs both fundamental analysis *and* technical analysis for good reason. The primary objective in business is to make more money with less effort; therefore, dynamic analysis is the most efficient use of my time. One of our objectives in employing this strategy is to work less than one hour per week, so buying and selling stocks like Fortescue will be too much hard work as they would require daily monitoring. On the other hand, waiting around for shares in Telstra to start rising is also a grossly inefficient use of time and money. Let's take another look at the chart of CSL (see figure 6.10).

Figure 6.9: Fortescue share price volatility

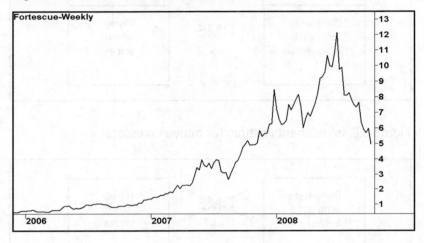

Figure 6.10: CSL steadily rising share price

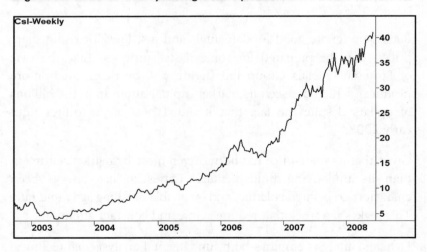

The price of CSL shares hasn't risen steadily over five years because of takeover rumours, market speculation and other unpredictable short-term factors that affect opinion. However, it has risen steadily over time because of its sound fundamentals and good future prospects. The previous chart of CSL is a weekly one and only requires checking on a weekly basis. Owning CSL shares for the past several years would have meant spending about 10 seconds per week glancing at this chart.

What we are doing as active investors is riding on the coat-tails of the fundamentalists. Furthermore, by choosing to operate in a weekly timeframe we go a long way towards filtering out the short-term unpredictable factors that affect the crowd's opinion.

In table 6.1, the various factors that affect opinion are categorised and prioritised by their timeframe and degree of significance. Although this list is by no means comprehensive, it includes the major factors that drive share prices either up or down. A more thorough explanation of each is provided in chapter 11.

Table 6.1: timeframe of factors that affect opinion

Factor	Timeframe
Fundamentals	Medium-term
Global factors	Medium-term
Macro economics	Medium-term
Market cycles	Long-term
News and rumours	Short-term
Gambling and speculation	Short-term

Buy low, sell high

Active investing flies in the face of the common advice, 'buy low, sell high'. This concept causes the majority of market participants to own shares which are *not* rising in price. 'Buy low' makes a lot of sense when it comes to buying tangible assets but when buying and selling shares for profit 'buy low, sell high' ignores the prevailing market sentiment and relies on prediction rather than probability.

Brokers will often recommend buying shares when prices fall. But the folly in this was driven home for me many years ago when I received a phone call from one of my brokers when the price of Lend Lease Corporation's shares collapsed in early 2001. My broker suggested that shares were at a bargain price and I should buy *now*. The share price had dropped from just over $22 to $17 on the back of bad news (see figure 6.11). But would the share price fall any lower than $17?

Figure 6.11: Lend Lease share price collapse

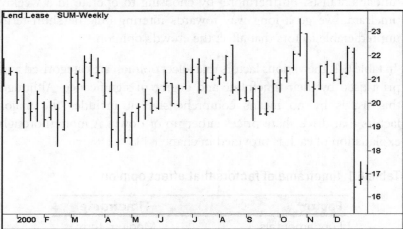

Nearly three months on and 'oops', the price drops a further $2, as shown in figure 6.12.

Figure 6.12: Lend Lease share price, three months on

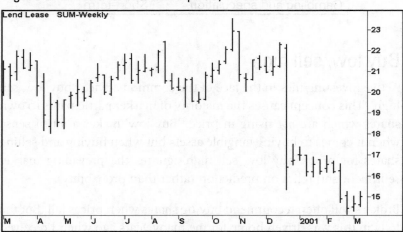

What this example illustrates is that there is no such thing as a bargain share price. The price of a share is only ever the precise value that market participants collectively place on it at any particular moment in time. What the broker was really saying is that market sentiment is abnormally low and should improve from this point on. Surely $15 is the low and I should buy now. Lend Lease's share price will surely rise from this level. Wrong again (see figure 6.13).

Figure 6.13: Lend Lease share price plummets further

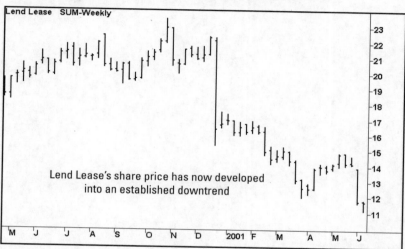

The problem with this approach is that there is no telling when sentiment is likely to improve. The broker has engaged in a guessing game of predicting market sentiment. Or is the stockbroker advising me to buy now because it would be in his best interests?

If a share price is rising then market sentiment is positive and if the share price is falling then market sentiment is negative. Hence, buy a rising share, sell a falling share. The broker's recommendation to buy because Lend Lease shares are at a low price is clearly flawed in its logic. Highs and lows can only be spotted with the benefit of hindsight and attempting to apply the theory of 'buy low, sell high' in the stock market would involve travelling forward in time.

However, by employing dynamic analysis, you are observing historical data and dealing largely in facts. Leave prediction to those who want to spend their time searching for so-called bargain-priced shares. We simply want to profit from having the balance of probability working in our favour. I am not trying to be clever, nor seeking perfection—just profits.

Chapter 7

Let the hunt begin

Fallacy: it's time in the market, not timing the market

Now that we have the conceptual side of our market strategy locked down, we must put the whole process into practice. Always bear in mind, though, that the most critical part of the process is already behind us. A market strategy based on sound concepts, but with poor or inaccurate execution, always beats a market approach that is based on flawed concepts but executed with high precision. In other words, even crawling in the right direction beats running in the wrong direction.

How we employ dynamic analysis will depend largely on our personal resources and skills. While some people will go out and spend thousands of dollars on the latest charting software, and happily pay a hundred dollars per month for ASX data, others who are less computer literate will feel a lot more comfortable just using the daily paper. To level the playing field for everyone, I distribute a weekly newsletter that contains all the necessary information for anybody who wants to be an active investor (see page 212).

Throughout the next several chapters, I will refer to the techniques and indicators I use in the newsletter, as well as other, simpler alternatives. While it is important for all of us to understand the concepts behind the techniques we employ, mastering finer technical details is of less importance.

Blue-chip companies with good fundamentals

Our search for trading opportunities begins with finding blue-chip companies with good fundamentals. When I needed to use a precise definition of 'blue chip' for my first book, *Charting in a Nutshell*, I was astonished to discover that almost nobody knew what it was. I thought it was the top 150 companies by market capitalisation, one of my brokers thought it was the top 200 companies, and there was no precise definition in my personal library of over 50 books on the stock market.

After I'd rung nearly a dozen people and spent half the day thumbing through my book collection, common sense finally prevailed with my publisher ringing the Australian Securities Exchange and putting the question to them. The answer is, according to the ASX, the top 500 companies by market capitalisation. So in a single pass we have narrowed the number of trading opportunities down to 500.

The next step is a little trickier, and definitely more involved, as we start to seek out only those companies with good fundamentals. By good fundamentals, I mean companies that have good financials, sound management, a sustained track record of profits, and promising future prospects. We now come up against the problem of defining a set of acceptable fundamental benchmarks. If the experts can't agree on what a good price/earnings ratio is, then how are we supposed to do it?

Ben Graham, the father of financial analysis, insisted on a price earnings ratio no higher than 25, and asset backing of least 66 per cent of the market valuation of the company. Do we adopt his benchmarks, or do we look to present-day financial analysts who are more in tune with today's prevailing economic conditions and industrial climate? What's alarming is the realisation that managing our portfolio in less than one hour per week is looking like a pipe dream if we have to individually assess the fundamentals of 500 companies, and repeat the process at least once a year.

However, thinking as a business person, my answer is to delegate the task to somebody else. Remember the mountain of information that our friend Douglas from the Traders Club was buried under? Among it is the fundamental company research of others who supposedly know a lot more than I do about reading financial reports, interpreting financial ratios, and so on. So, we'll let them do the hard work for us and we'll concentrate on the task at hand — dynamic analysis.

There are programs, books and websites that contain, in summarised form, the precise information we're after. One such source is Martin Roth's series of *Top Stocks* books, which is published annually by Wrightbooks. Each book in the series contains 100 of the most fundamentally sound blue-chip stocks for a particular year. The selection process is based on Roth's personal fundamental criteria, which are explained in the preface of each book. Roth is a financial analyst with over three decades of experience and every year he saves me thousands of hours of work by compressing everything I want to know into a book which costs me the measly sum of $39.95. If his book sold for 10 times its current price, I'd still buy it, and gladly.

Of course, there are other sources of information, including a very powerful computer program called StockDoctor. StockDoctor is an Australian product developed and distributed by Lincoln Indicators in Melbourne. The program uses financial benchmarks developed by Dr Merv Lincoln, a financial analyst, to sift out what the program describes as 'star stocks'. Star stocks are public companies that are expected to outperform other similar stocks. By filtering out only star stocks that are in the top 500 companies by market capitalisation, that is, with a market capitalisation of $100 million or more, we have another list of trading possibilities.

We can shop around for other products similar to *Top Stocks* or StockDoctor, or we can do some research ourselves if we are so inclined. But whatever you decide to do, at the end of the day you should have a list of between 100 and 150 fundamentally sound blue-chip stocks, which we can then subject to further scrutiny.

Rate of return

Out of this pool of fundamentally sound blue-chip stocks we want to extract only those that have a rising share price. We also want to compare those with rising share prices by quantitatively analysing how fast their share prices are rising over time. Consider the chart of company A (figure 7.1). At the beginning of August the share price was 60 cents, and at the end of February it was $2.10. The line covers a time span of seven months. So, the share price rose $1.50 in seven months.

Figure 7.1: upward trend in company A

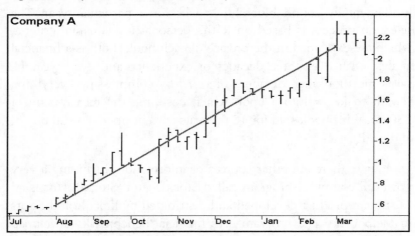

Now consider the chart of company B in figure 7.2. At the beginning of November the share price was $10.00, and by the end of March it was $12.00. The line covers a time span of five months. So, the share price rose $2.00 in five months.

Both these shares are obviously in an uptrend and on the face of it company B appears to have performed better, given that its share price rose $2.00 in five months while company A's share price only rose $1.50 over seven months. But in fact, the trend in company A was far more profitable because there was a greater proportional increase in the share price over time. However, in order to see this we have to analyse the proportional change in price, rather than the actual change in price.

Figure 7.2: upward trend in company B

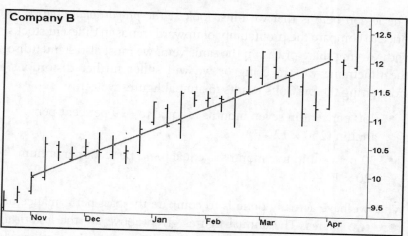

Proportional increase in the share price of company A

Assume that you bought shares in company A at 60 cents at the start of August.

- Seven months later, the share price has risen to $2.10, an increase of $1.50.
- Therefore, the proportional increase on 60 cents is 2.5 (1.50 ÷ 0.60).
- Converting 2.5 to a percentage we get 250 per cent.
- Therefore, the share price rose 250 per cent in seven months.

Proportional increase in the share price of company B

Assume that you bought shares in company B at $10.00 at the start of November.

- Five months later, the share price has risen to $12.00, an increase of $2.00.

- Therefore, the proportional increase on $10.00 is 0.2 (2.00 ÷ 10.00).

- Converting 0.2 to a percentage we get 20 per cent.

- Therefore, the share price rose 20 per cent in five months.

The lesson here is that we must look at the *proportional* change in price to compare the profitability of upward trends in different stocks with varying share prices. In the same vein, we must also standardise the timeframe we are using or we will suffer further distortions. Converting the previous results to annual figures we get:

- 250 per cent in seven months is equal to 429 per cent per annum (250 × 12 ÷ 7)

- 20 per cent in five months is equal to 48 per cent per annum (20 × 12 ÷ 5).

What we have actually done is to compare the past performance of these two shares. The annual figures given above are the *historical* annual rates of return for companies A and B because they are based on the share prices from the beginning of their respective trends. We now have to accept the reality that we can't travel back in time. Company A's annual rate of return of 429 per cent would only apply to us if we had bought shares at 60 cents, back in August. Let's take another look at the chart of company A (see figure 7.3).

Figure 7.3: company A share price chart

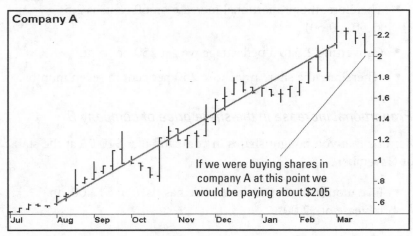

The reality is that we can only buy shares in it using the price on the right hand edge of chart. Regrettably, this higher purchase price will have a negative affect on our annual rate of return, as follows.

- Increase in the price of company A over the previous seven months is $1.50.

- Proportional change in price over seven months using $2.05 is 0.73 (1.50 ÷ 2.05).

- Converting to a percentage we get 73 per cent.

- Converting to an annual rate of return we get 125 per cent (73 × 12 ÷ 7).

Therefore, based on the current trend in company A and the current share price, the current annual rate of return that we can expect if the trend remains constant is 125 per cent. It may not be 429 per cent, but 125 per cent is not too shabby either. So whenever we measure the rate of return of share prices for comparative purposes we must use:

- the proportional increase in share price over time

- a standardised timeframe for comparison, for example, one year

- the current share price as our frame of reference, that is, our expected purchase price.

Only when we have applied all the above criteria are we able to compare apples with apples.

Dealing with the curvy bits

A further complication we need to consider is that not all of the shares we want to analyse will be progressing in a straight line. In the case of either company A or company B, the trends could be defined using a straight line. Unfortunately, we will encounter a lot of share price charts which will be banana-shaped, such as that of company C (figure 7.4, overleaf).

If we were to measure the rate of return for company C by using the price change over one year, we would come up with a different answer than if we had only used the price change over the previous three months. To solve this dilemma we must employ a method that is a compromise between these two extremes.

Figure 7.4: company C share price chart

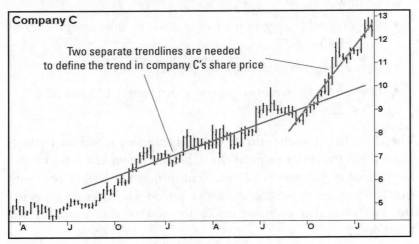

The following chart of company C's share price (figure 7.5) shows a line of linear regression that is generated using one year of price activity. In other words, a line of best fit over the past one year period.

Figure 7.5: company C share price chart with line of linear regression

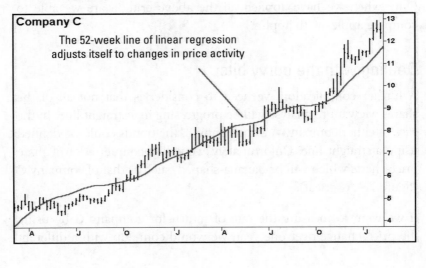

It is not necessary to understand the mathematics behind linear regression, but simply to understand that it is used to find a 'line of best fit' over a given period. Most popular charting programs have a linear regression function.

Now that we have a smooth unbroken line that depicts the change in price over the previous 12 months, we can use it to measure the annual rate of return. We can measure the change in price, over a given period, of a 52-week line of linear regression to find the annual rate of return, as follows:

- value of the 52-week line of linear regression today is 11.67
- value of the 52-week line of linear regression six months ago was 9.06 (six months is a compromise between three months and one year)
- current share price is 12.37
- annual rate of return is 0.21(11.67 − 9.06 ÷ 12.37)
- annualised by doubling and converted to a percentage you get 42 per cent.

Given the non-linear nature of share price movements, we are forced into this somewhat convoluted solution to the problem. But thanks to charting software, we simply have to reduce our calculations into a formula that can be understood by a computer and it will do the work for us.

'Rate of return' indicator

The 'rate of return' or RoR indicator, can be used to automatically calculate the annual rate of return of shares. If we use the method described above to build our indicator it would look like the chart shown in figure 7.6 (overleaf). The RoR indicator is a classic example of how technology can be employed to make our job easier. It is the brainchild of our needs.

The RoR indicator pictured is returning a figure of 42.43 per cent, which coincides with our manual calculations. Although we can achieve different results by sampling the change in price over different periods, it is only imperative that we adhere to our original concept of rate of return and that we are consistent in our approach. We are interested in comparing different trends rather than trying to come up with a perfect method that gives us perfect answers.

Figure 7.6: price chart showing RoR indicator

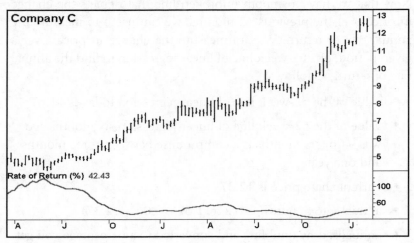

Thanks to the RoR indicator, we now have the ability to analyse our pool of fundamentally sound blue-chip stocks by simply pressing a button. The share price chart for company D (figure 7.7) shows the RoR indicator with a horizontal line set at 20 per cent.

Figure 7.7: RoR indicator with horizontal line set at 20 per cent

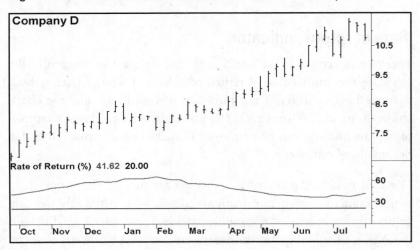

Most charting programs have a search capability, which allows us to filter out shares that don't meet our criteria. By setting our horizontal bar at 20 per cent, we can search through our fundamentally sound blue-chip stocks and eliminate any with an annual rate of return of less than 20 per cent. After we've performed this search, our pool of stocks will be reduced down to approximately 40 to 50 stocks, given normal market conditions. So we now have 40 to 50 fundamentally sound blue-chip stocks where the share price is rising by at least 20 per cent per annum.

We can adjust this benchmark to control the number of stocks found by our search. We want to narrow our list down to about 40 to 50 stocks, as we can deal with this number on an individual basis. The steps we have undertaken thus far, although simple enough, are the most important part of the overall process. From this point forward we are effectively finetuning the whole operation.

In fact, if you actually tried to lose money using this pool of fundamentally sound stocks with rising share prices, you would find it very difficult indeed. The balance of probability is now weighted in your favour.

New trends and old trends

Looking back at the chart of company C, we can see that the rate of return is highest during the early part of the trend and that it diminishes as the trend progresses. Although it is not essential, we do want to try to get on board trends while there is still some mileage left in them.

In other words, if we set our search criterion at 20 per cent and we buy a stock with a rate of return of 22 per cent, then its rate of return could fall below our criteria of 20 per cent in a very short space of time. We need to set an 'entry' rate of return that will ensure we don't buy into a tired trend. To demonstrate, the chart of company D, shown in figure 7.8 (overleaf), now includes a second horizontal bar set at 30 per cent.

If we use a rate of return of 30 per cent as a benchmark for buying a stock, and 20 per cent as the benchmark for holding the stock, then we will avoid buying into trends that are becoming too tired. At the current rate of return for company D we are prepared to keep holding it but we would not be prepared to buy it unless the rate of return increased. Furthermore, if the rate of return falls below 20 per cent then we will sell, because if our money isn't earning at least 20 per cent per annum we need to find a better home for it.

Figure 7.8: RoR indicator with second horizontal line set at 30 per cent

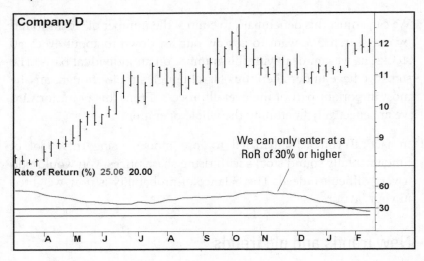

The rate of return will also fall below 20 per cent if the trend moves sideways for a prolonged period—another unacceptable situation. Mind you, it is normal for blue-chip share prices to move sideways for several months at a time (take company D from October to February for example), and we must rely on the RoR indicator to evaluate this behaviour rather than trusting in our gut feelings or fallible instincts.

Ready-made market: liquidity

Earlier I stated that running an s-store business meant having ready-made customers and no supply problems. By this I meant that there are always shares available for me to buy, and there will always be someone prepared to buy them from me when I want to sell. This is true provided I ensure that the marketplace has plenty of actively involved market participants buying and selling particular shares. Unfortunately, not all the top 500 companies, that is, blue-chip stocks, enjoy active trading.

Each week shares are bought and sold and the Australian Securities Exchange reports on the number of shares that are turned over, as well as the price information. The number of shares that are bought and sold each week, is referred to as the 'volume of shares traded'. Trading volume is listed in the share price tables of all daily newspapers and often appears as a histogram at the bottom of price charts.

Before buying into a stock we need to check the volume to ensure that there is a good supply of shares for us to purchase and that there are plenty of customers for us to sell to when the time comes for us to do so. The following chart of BHP (figure 7.9) has plenty of trading volume and so BHP is said to be a stock with good liquidity. On the other hand, Energy Metals Limited (figure 7.10, overleaf) has very poor liquidity. Note how there are weeks when the price barely moves at all. By contrast, BHP's price activity is much more fluid.

Figure 7.9: BHP share price chart

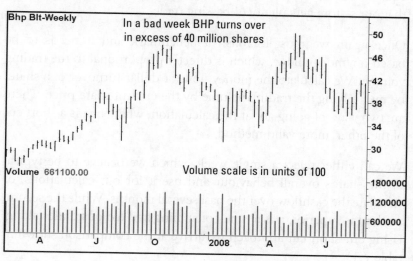

Figure 7.10: Energy Metals share turnover

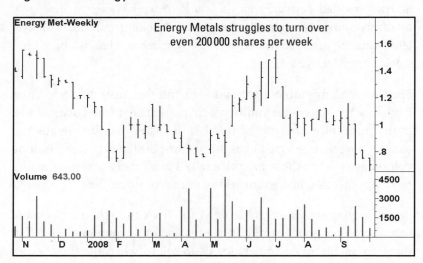

If we were trying to buy shares in a company like Energy Metals, we would find a shortage of sellers, and when we were ready to sell our shares there would probably be a shortage of willing buyers. We would find ourselves in the same situation as a store owner with no customers. Store owners say, 'Location, location, location'. Our equivalent catch cry is, 'Liquidity, liquidity, liquidity'. We must ensure that our s-store gets plenty of passing trade.

Once again we must establish a benchmark and it needs to be based on 'money flow', which is directly proportional to the trading volume. We calculate the money flow, or dollar turnover of a share, by multiplying the trading volume by the current share price. There are two ways of going about the calculation, where one is a short cut of the other, more valid method.

We can either select a single week, which we believe to be typical of the share's overall behaviour and use it for our calculations, or calculate the cashflow over the past several months. While the second method is superior, it is a time-consuming and tedious undertaking. Using our short cut approach we arrive at the comparison shown in table 7.1.

The liquidity or money flow of BHP is totally acceptable, whereas that of Energy Metals is not. In my experience, a sensible benchmark for liquidity would be an average money flow of at least $1 million per week.

Table 7.1: comparison between BHP and Energy Metals

	BHP	Energy Metals
Trading volume	60 million	100 000
Price	$40.00	$1.00
Money flow	$2.4 billion/wk	$100 000/wk

Bringing it all together

Figure 7.11 shows the linear RoR indicator I use to generate the data in my weekly newsletter. It tests and measures all the criteria covered in this chapter. The linear RoR indicator makes the whole task of searching for shares much faster and easier by incorporating all our search criteria into a single indicator. It checks for an annual rate of return equal to or higher than 20 per cent, and money flow of at least $13 million per quarter (13 weeks). It switches itself 'off' if either of these conditions isn't met, or if the price activity moves sideways for a prolonged period of time. As I stated earlier, there is no single correct approach for employing dynamic analysis but a range of different ways in which we can apply its concepts.

Figure 7.11: RoR indicator used to measure required criteria

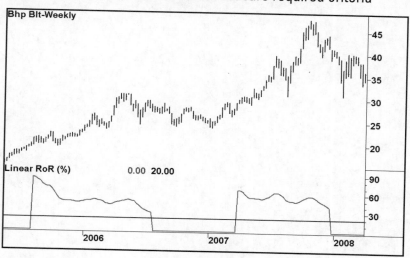

Similarly, the benchmarks I have used in this chapter are not set in stone. Although they are the result of comprehensive analysis and testing, they will become obsolete at some point in the future when market conditions change. If the market slows down over time then we will have to lower our benchmarks in order to find enough trading opportunities, and the opposite applies if we enter a bull market. Realistically, we accept that we'll see periods of both bull and bear markets in the future. It is the concepts on which we base our strategy that remain constant.

Chapter 8

Separating the wheat from the chaff

Cut your losses and let your profits run

The previous chapter dealt primarily with quantitative analysis and produced a short list of 40 to 50 trading candidates by testing and measuring price and volume activity. If this is all that is required of us, then we should be able to automate the entire process and live happily ever after. However, in order to lessen the impact of short-term factors that affect opinion such as rumours, short-term speculators, and so on, we need to ensure that a company's fundamentals are the main driving force behind the market dynamic. The specific market dynamic we are trying to isolate is depicted in figure 8.1.

Figure 8.1: market dynamic with good fundamentals

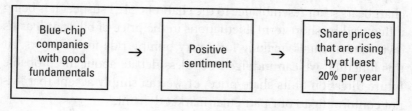

Blue-chip companies with good fundamentals	→	Positive sentiment	→	Share prices that are rising by at least 20% per year

Ensuring that our blue-chip companies have good fundamentals doesn't necessarily mean that those fundamentals are the sole cause for rising share prices. We must perform qualitative analysis to eliminate as many unpredictable short-term factors as we possibly can. Once again, consider the chart of CSL (figure 8.2). The share price is rising steadily over time and is largely unaffected by short-term factors.

Figure 8.2: CSL rising share price

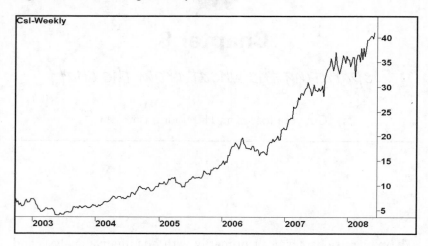

We want to pinpoint shares like CSL that will keep us smiling for years, doing very little work to manage our portfolio. Therefore, we must seek out shares that are similar in nature, insofar as they are devoid of volatility. The key thing to look for is shares that are rising steadily over time, with steadily being the key word. Fundamentals affect share prices over the long-term and don't cause price activity to behave violently. Santos Limited is also a blue-chip stock with good fundamentals, but its share price is influenced by factors other than its fundamentals, as illustrated by its erratic price activity (figure 8.3). Technically, Santos fits all our search criteria but its price chart bears scant resemblance to the chart of CSL. I suspect it is being influenced by short-term fluctuations in the price of oil as well as its own fundamentals, making for a very bumpy ride for investors. At this juncture, we can indulge in endless debate about the probable future direction of its share price, or we can simply accept that it is not conforming to our particular market dynamic.

Figure 8.3: Santos fluctuating share price

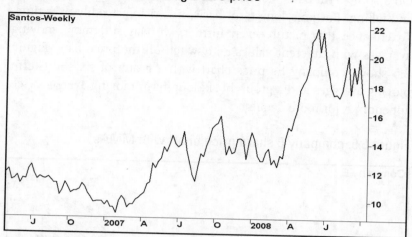

Multiple moving averages

Our assessment of CSL and Santos is based wholly on our qualitative interpretation of their respective price charts. Even though we only need to examine about 50 shares, we can make the job a lot easier by using a method that will visually isolate the effect of both short-term and long-term factors.

The chart of company E (figure 8.4) has two moving averages—a short-term average of five weeks and a long-term average of 30 weeks.

Figure 8.4: company E share price chart

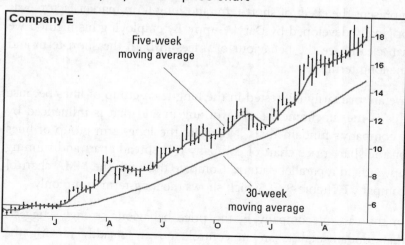

On a short-term basis, company E's share price is repeatedly rising and falling. But on a long-term basis, it is rising steadily over time. To enhance this picture even further, we can add more moving averages with different values and switch off the price bars. Figure 8.5 shows company E's price chart with a group of six short-term moving averages and a group of six long-term moving averages (see appendix A for more details).

Figure 8.5: company E share price chart with MMAs

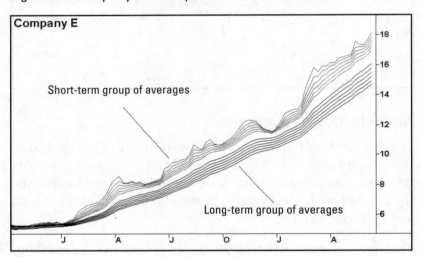

Chartists refer to this type of chart as a 'multiple moving averages' or MMA chart. The technique of having two groups of averages to represent the effect of short-term and long-term market factors was originally developed by Daryl Guppy. By employing his method we can clearly see the behaviour of prices in both the short-term and the long-term.

We are primarily interested in the long-term group of lines because this is the timeframe we are working in and that is influenced by a company's fundamentals. Note that the long-term group of lines on the share price chart of company E is spread apart and running upwards in a parallel pattern. Compare this with the MMA chart of company F (figure 8.6), which shows the long-term group only.

In the case of company E, the price behaviour strongly suggests that fundamentalists are in control and are steadily moving the share price up over time. In contrast, if we assume that company F has good fundamentals, then fundamentals are not the key factor influencing its share price. Short-term factors, whatever they may be, are having a large impact. Note how the long-term group of averages is constantly compressing and expanding as the price activity moves up and down.

Figure 8.6: company F share price chart showing only long-term moving averages

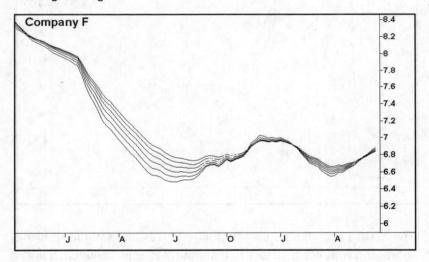

If price activity moves in the same direction over time then the long-term group of lines will separate and eventually establish themselves in a parallel formation as they have in company E's chart. This is one of the characteristics we are looking for when we observe MMA charts.

The long-term group of lines must be either spreading apart or moving parallel to each other but they must not be compressing and coming together. Once we're satisfied with the behaviour of the long-term group we can turn our attention to the short-term group of lines. The following chart of company E's share price (figure 8.7, overleaf) shows only the short-term group of lines.

We expect the short-term group of lines to compress and expand over time. This is normal behaviour for any share, and is indicative of the influence of short-term factors and frequent profit-taking by short-term market participants. We want to ensure that short-term factors are having little to no impact on us and that they never become strong enough to overpower the longer term factors, namely, good fundamentals. To this end, we want to see the short-term group of averages bouncing along in a consistent and uniform pattern, as is the case with company E.

Figure 8.7: company E share price chart showing only short-term moving averages

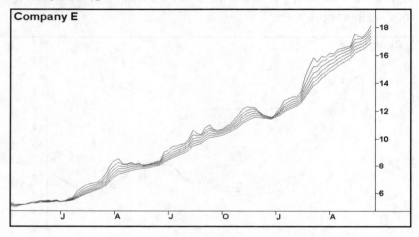

The MMA chart of company G (figure 8.8) is an example showing short- and long-term factors that are fairly evenly weighted. This is not a situation we want to buy into—literally.

Figure 8.8: company G evenly weighted MMA chart

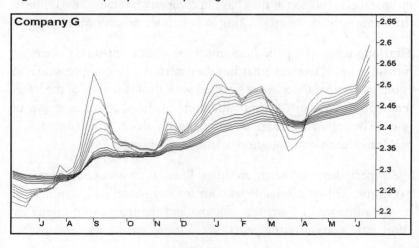

If short-term factors are capable of taking control of the share price, then we will observe this on an MMA chart by looking for crossovers between the short- and long-term groups of lines. This type of volatility indicates that the balance of control is fairly even.

To summarise, the qualities we are looking for are:

- the long-term group must be spreading apart or running parallel with each other

- the long-term group must be pointing upwards

- the straighter the long-term group of lines are, the better

- the short-term group must be behaving in a consistent, repetitive manner

- the short-term group must not cross into the long-term group.

If we seek out shares with the above qualities, then we should enjoy long-term trends like the ones shown in figures 8.9, 8.10 (overleaf), 8.11 (overleaf), 8.12 (on page 111) and 8.13 (on page 111). Basically, if we work hard today, we won't have to work at all tomorrow.

JB Hi-Fi Limited's share price rose steadily from $6 to $16 over a 15-month period.

Figure 8.9: JB Hi-Fi MMA chart

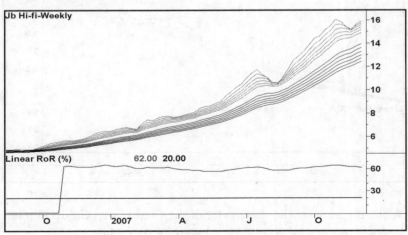

The linear RoR indicator captured this steadily rising 12-month trend in the share price of David Jones Limited.

Figure 8.10: David Jones MMA chart

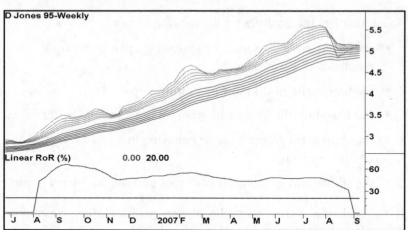

The share price of McMillan Shakespeare Limited rose from under $2 to just over $5 during this trend, which lasted nearly two years.

Figure 8.11: McMillan MMA chart

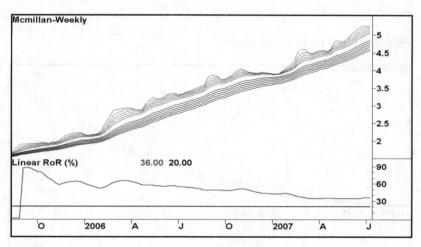

While the trend in the share price of the Credit Corp Group Limited hesitated on several occasions, it lasted for two years.

Figure 8.12: Creditcorp MMA chart

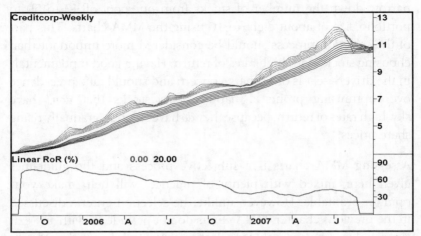

Note that when the share price of Melbourne IT Limited hesitated in the third quarter of 2006, the linear RoR indicator started to drop. Had the market hesitated much longer then the linear RoR would have eventually dropped below 20 per cent, and the short-term group of averages would have touched the long-term group of averages, with either of these events invalidating the trend.

Figure 8.13: Melbourne IT MMA chart

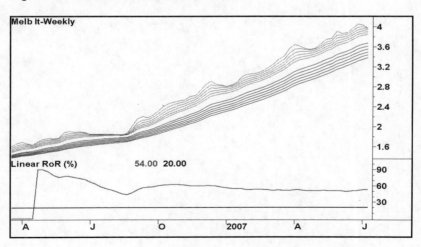

This is the final phase of the hunt and we should now be able to narrow down the number of stocks from our pool of 40 to 50 to portfolio size of about eight to 10 using the MMA charts. This part of the selection process should be considered more important than choosing stocks with high rates of return. Having good fundamentals in the driver's seat is of primary concern and should take precedence over optimising profits. I happily own stocks that *don't* have sky-high rates of return, because they *do* have smooth, gradually rising share prices.

Assessing MMA charts is a subjective process and the guidelines given here, mixed with plenty of practice, will help make your opinion profitable. However, unlike the selection criteria discussed in the previous chapter, MMA charts do not provide us with any exit signals; they are used only for selecting which stocks we should buy. There are better and less ambiguous techniques for knowing when to sell. Interestingly, this is where most of us get into trouble, as we'll see in the next chapter.

Chapter 9

Buy, hold or sell? That is the question

No-one ever went broke taking profits

I am an indecisive person at the best of times so when someone else's opinion presents me with even more options and variables to deal with, my ability to make decisions is hampered even further. Many experienced traders do not seek the counsel of other traders for this very reason—it only introduces more variables into the equation. To demonstrate, let's look at a simple maths problem with only one variable.

$$2 + X = 5$$

The answer to a one-variable equation can be found simply and easily but as we introduce more variables, the process becomes more difficult.

$$2X + 3Y - Z = 5 \qquad X - 2Y + 2Z = 3 \qquad 3X + Y + Z = 8$$

The more variables, the more difficult the task becomes. This is true of any decision-making process. A mathematician would solve the above problems by eliminating variables one by one. In the marketplace we are presented with a minefield of variables. Rather than eliminate them one by one, most of us go actively looking for more, creating a prison of knowledge like the one Douglas from my Traders Club built for himself. Thankfully, the dynamic analysis process described in chapter 6 goes a long way towards narrowing down the number of variables we have to deal with. We will now eliminate further potential for indecision by mechanising the process of when to buy, when to hold and when to sell.

When to buy

Once we've chosen our portfolio of around eight to 10 stocks, we are at the final stage of making the decision to enter the market. This is where our 'space monkey' is going to climb into the driver's seat. It must have a set of very simple and completely unambiguous instructions to follow. We want to optimise our market entry by buying into the market during a pullback in the price activity (see figure 9.1), but we don't want to rely on guesswork.

Figure 9.1: optimal times for market entry

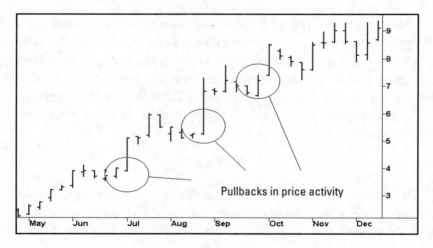

We must ensure that the process is completely mechanical and there is no room for personal discretion. This is not the moment to question strategy or deal with unknown variables. Consider the chart of company H (figure 9.2), which has a 13-week line of linear regression placed on it.

Figure 9.2: company H share price chart

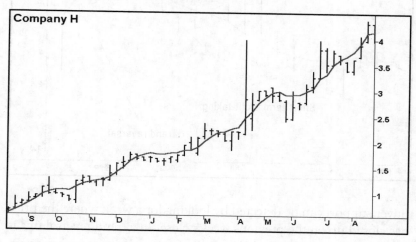

We could create the above chart just as easily with pen and paper and draw a straight line right through the middle of the price activity. The purpose of the exercise is to separate the peaks from the troughs. The peaks are moments in the short-term cycle where the bulls or optimists are in control and buying the share price up in a rally period. The troughs are created by short-term profit-taking. We want to enter the market during the profit-taking period, when the price activity drops below the line of linear regression.

Psychologically, most of us are more inclined to chase a running market and we lose interest in the whole exercise when the price activity begins to retreat. That's why we need a monkey in the driver's seat instead of us; from this point on, our personal psychology will be in direct conflict with our actions. However, we're not going to buy the stock when the price activity is *actually* falling. Any period during which the price activity is falling, could just as easily be a break in the long-term trend as opposed to a period of short-term profit-taking. We need a way of differentiating between the two. The difference is the re-appearance of buyers in the marketplace and the resulting price support they provide. Consider figure 9.3 (overleaf) where we can see several pullbacks and a complete trend reversal.

Figure 9.3: pullbacks versus trend reversal

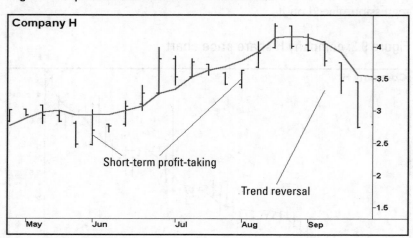

Figure 9.4: minor uptrend within a major uptrend

Buyer support can be detected by looking for a week where the price has closed up on the previous week's close. In a trend reversal this is far less likely to occur and by waiting for it to happen we can avoid buying into a trend at the start of a major reversal. Once we have witnessed buyer support, we then want to make our move and buy the stock during the following week. We are fine-tuning our entry by getting on board at the start of a minor uptrend within a major uptrend, as shown in figure 9.4.

Figure 9.4: minor uptrend within a major uptrend

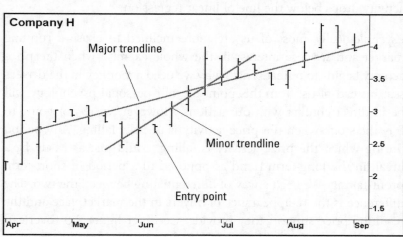

When to sell

Probably the toughest question for most of us is when to sell our shares. While logic often tells us to cut our losses or that the trend is over, either our self-esteem doesn't want to cope with a loss or we have become emotionally attached to the stock. Rather than work on improving our self-esteem or becoming more objective, we seek to alter our logic by finding reasons to justify hanging on to the stock.

To prevent this from happening we need to employ a totally unambiguous solution. This time, we need to identify the point at which a falling share price is a trend reversal, as opposed to a pullback in price due to short-term profit-taking. Looking again at the chart of company H (figure 9.5), we can observe the overall trend to get an idea of the difference between a temporary pullback in price activity and a full-blown trend reversal.

Figure 9.5: company H share price chart showing pullback versus trend reversal

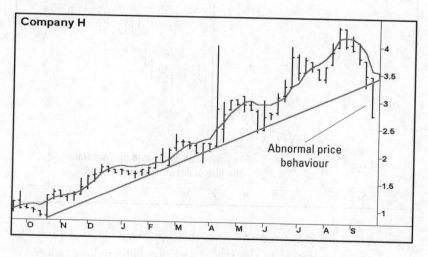

By simply drawing a trendline that touches the lower extremes of price activity, we are able to see that the final break in the trend is very much out of character with earlier price behaviour. I have included the 13-week line of linear regression in the chart so that the 'buy zone' can be clearly seen.

The supportive trendline that is set according to the behaviour of previous price activity is representative of our tolerance towards a falling share price. We can use it as a stop loss, which means that should the share price close below this line, we will sell the share the following week. There is no ambiguity in this statement but the door is open to any naughty space monkeys who want to tinker and reposition the trendline. This is not an uncommon occurrence if the monkey is also the chief engineer who placed the trendline in the first place.

An alternative to using a moveable trendline is to create an envelope based on the 13-week line of linear regression. This is achieved by displacing the line of linear regression by a proportional factor, the result of which is shown in the chart of company H (figure 9.6).

Figure 9.6: company H share price chart with line of linear regression displaced by 20 per cent

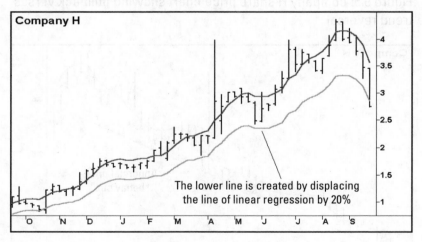

However, there is a problem with this approach. Notice how our lower line is retreating in sympathy with the falling share price. We can move a stop loss price up as the trend progresses, but we must not allow it to retreat as price activity falls. One of the golden rules of trading is not to widen your stop loss under any circumstances. The lower line in the following chart (figure 9.7) is prevented from falling in sympathy with the price activity. This causes it to 'flatline' during pullbacks.

Figure 9.7: the benefit of maintaining a steady stop loss

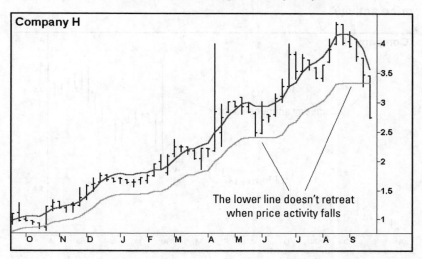

We now have a monkey-proof stop loss that provides us with a totally unambiguous selling signal. When the closing price (the tick to the right of the bar) is below the lower line, we must sell our shares during the following week. Now it's time to deal with our greed.

When to hold and when to take profits

In the chart of company H, shown in figure 9.8 (overleaf), we can see a week where the price activity was completely out of character and spiked upwards. This actually happened in reaction to an announcement by the company.

This is a classic example of how news can have a short-term impact on price activity. Most experienced traders avoid using the sophisticated and complex indicators that have come into being over the last few decades because they can get all the information they need by just observing the raw price data.

In the chart you can see the long-term crowd at work, gradually moving the share price upwards over time. In contrast, the price suddenly spikes up out of its normal trading range, and almost doubles in one week. However, the longer-term market participants quickly regain control and price activity returns to its earlier trading range.

119

Figure 9.8: company H share price chart showing unusual price activity

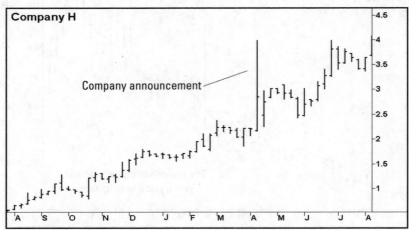

We can equate this event to a small crowd of rowdy youths at a football match whose behaviour deteriorates over time. At some point, this small crowd within a larger crowd will reach the tolerance point of the larger crowd and be pulled back into line. The market participants who reacted to the company announcement by buying up the share price don't have the same monetary force behind them as the longer-term market participants. So in the capital democracy of the stock market, where $1 equals one vote, the long-term view that controls the bulk of the money wins out over the shorter term view.

The short-term crowd, though, have left their mark on the market and you can see how the price activity takes on a slightly steeper gradient following the announcement. The smaller crowd has been absorbed by the larger crowd. Price activity can be shifted suddenly either up or down, but it will remain within the tolerances of the larger crowd if it doesn't disperse.

Knowing that the larger crowd, who form their opinions using long-term factors, will probably overpower those using short-term factors, we can exploit this type of situation. The upper line in the chart of company H (figure 9.9) is created by displacing the line of linear regression upwards by a proportional factor of 25 per cent.

Figure 9.9: company H share price chart with line of linear regression displaced upwards by 25 per cent

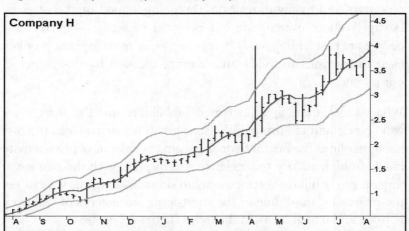

The upper and lower lines define the tolerance of the larger, long-term crowd. In a similar way to our stop loss technique, the upper line tells us when to sell our shares and take profits. If price activity moves above the upper line, then we know on the balance of probability that it will return to its earlier trading range. This is the ideal time to take quick profits. We always have the option of re-entering the market when price activity dips back below the central line of linear regression.

Let's revisit our business objectives for a moment. We are aiming for an annual return on our total capital of at least 20 per cent per annum. We can refine this objective by also defining an upper limit. Being realistic, and bearing in mind that the higher the return, the higher the risk, I am more than content with an upper limit of 50 per cent.

By setting an upper limit before entering the market, we are far more likely to make a realistic decision that won't be based in any way on short-term market performance or on any degree of irrational exuberance. While it is nice to watch the shares you own double in price over a period of a few weeks, it is dangerous to base your longer term expectations on this type of market behaviour.

A 100 per cent increase in price over two weeks is the equivalent of a 2600 per cent increase per annum, which is well in excess of our objectives and totally unrealistic. Designing a good market strategy is largely about overcoming our personal weakness—greed. Most people are inherently greedy by nature, so we must give the monkey clear instructions to follow that are not dictated by this aspect of our psyche.

What's more, there is an increased probability that the share price will reverse and fall through the stop loss if it has managed to cross the upper line. The sawtooth or zigzagging behaviour of price activity has a strong tendency to accelerate and increase with the passage of time. It rarely builds in tempo only to slow down again. We can see the increasing amplitude in the short-term movements of company H prior to the final break in the trend (figure 9.10).

Figure 9.10: company H share price chart showing break in trend

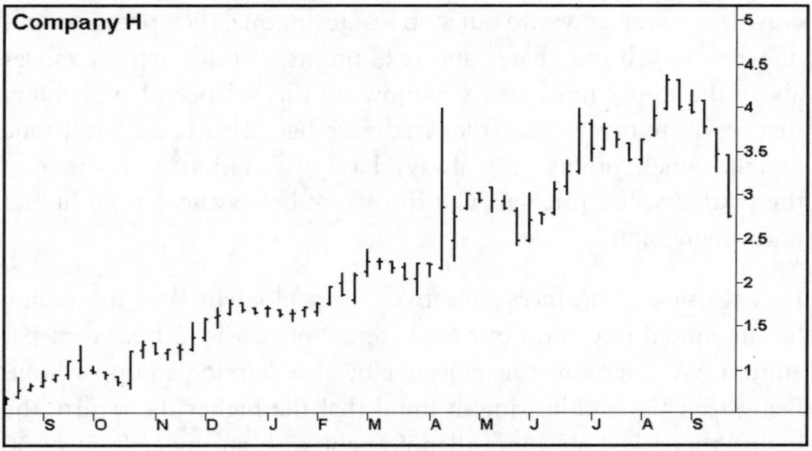

Price volatility

Our market strategy, as well as overcoming our psychological tendencies, must always work in harmony with the normal behaviour of price activity and the forces driving it. Trying to work against these forces is the equivalent of stepping in front of an express train. Every trend, whether it is up, down or sideways, is driven by a specific crowd with a unique personality.

So far in this chapter I have used just one example, company H. Furthermore, I have displaced the upper and lower lines to suit the behaviour of one particular trend, and the values I have used are unique to this trend alone. However, the following chart (figure 9.11) shows the result of using the same upper and lower displacements on a different trend, this time in company K.

Figure 9.11: company K share price chart

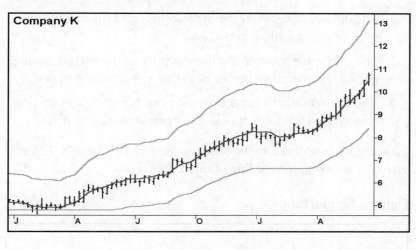

'Silly' is the word that springs to mind when looking at the chart of company K. The crowd behind this trend has a totally different personality to the crowd driving the upward trend in company H. So unless we want to 'curve fit' our upper and lower lines for every trend we decide to trade, we will have to find a more universal method of positioning the upper and lower lines.

The difference in price behaviour between these two upward trends is their volatility. To put it simply, the price movements in the trend of company H are proportionally greater than the price movements in company K. We can also see, by re-examining the charts, that the weekly trading range of company H is proportionally greater than that of company K.

So to solve this problem, the displacement of the upper and lower lines needs to be based on the proportional price movements and trading range of each individual share. Luckily, an American trader and author, J Welles Wilder, has already tackled and solved this problem for us.

Wilder developed the concept of 'true range', which defines the volatility of price activity, taking into account during any given trading period both the price range and price movements between trading periods. He defined true range as being the largest of three measurements.

1   The difference between the highest price and the lowest price of the current trading period.

2   The difference between the highest price of the current trading period and the closing price of the previous trading period.

3   The difference between the lowest price of the current trading period and the closing price of the previous trading period.

Looking at these three measurements on a chart (figure 9.12) will give us a better understanding of them.

Figure 9.12: true range

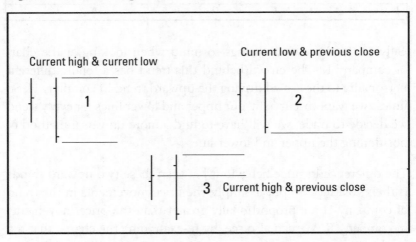

True range is based on the two most recent trading periods and is of little use to us if we are trying to measure price volatility over a longer period of time. We have to calculate the *average* true range in order to put the concept to practical use. We can select any period of time we like on which to base our calculations. Since our line of linear regression is based on 13 weeks, we should be consistent and use the same period.

The following charts of company H (figure 9.13) and company K (figure 9.14) have upper lines that are displaced by three times the 13-week average true range, and lower lines that are displaced by two and a half times the 13-week average true range.

Figure 9.13: company H share price chart using average true range concept

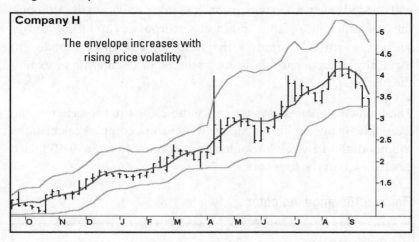

Figure 9.14: company K share price chart using average true range concept

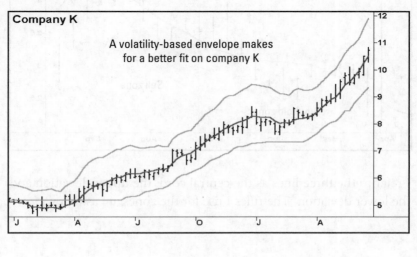

The reason for displacing the upper line by a slightly larger proportion than the lower line is that the line of linear regression tends to lag behind the most recent price activity. In an upward trend this causes it to be displaced slightly downwards.

The range indicator

The three lines we have constructed create what I refer to as the 'range indicator'. It defines four distinct areas or zones. Our actions will depend solely upon which zone the price activity is in. Although the construction of this indicator incorporates a bit of rocket science, it virtually removes the need for our space monkey to make any discretionary decisions at the point of entering or exiting the market.

The following chart shows the range indicator I use to generate the data tables in my weekly newsletter. It uses some complex calculations to smooth the 13-week line of linear regression. In figure 9.15 I have labeled each of the four zones.

Figure 9.15: range indicator

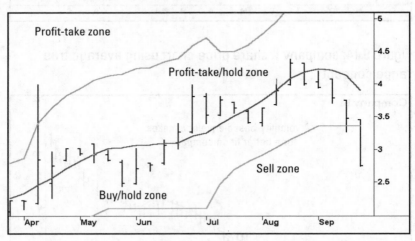

I refer to the three lines as the central cord, the upper deviation and the lower deviation. The rules I use for the zones are as follows:

Sell zone	*Mandatory*	**Sell** if the share price closes at the end of a week in this zone.
	Optional	**Sell** if the share price closes at the end of a day in this zone.
Buy/hold zone		**Buy** if the share price closes at the end of a week in this zone and the price is higher than the previous week's closing price. The purchase price must be between the lower deviation and the central cord. **Hold** if already owned.
Profit-take/ hold zone		**Hold** if the share price is in this zone or **take profits** if the position is up strongly, for example, sell half the position.
Profit-take zone	*Mandatory*	**Take profits** if the share price closes at the end of the week in this zone. In this instance, sell the entire position.
	Optional	**Take profits** if the share price is in this zone at any time.

The key to being successful lies in having a set of rules. If there is a problem with our rules then we can always change them. But a monkey without a set of rules will inevitably get up to mischief.

Chapter 10

Managing the losses makes you profitable

Diversification is the result of risk management—not vice versa

---

Risk management could just as easily be referred to as loss management. Successful market participants are successful because they focus on, and manage their losses. While fixating on profits is an enjoyable pastime, it will do little more than make you feel good for a time. The three key elements we can manage when we are buying and selling shares are:

- the balance of probability
- the scale of payouts, that is, the value of winning versus the cost of losing
- the size of our positions—how much we spend when we buy shares.

Although I don't want to confuse buying and selling shares with gambling in any way, it is helpful for the purposes of illustration to compare buying and selling shares with games of chance. At some point in time, most of us have played the simple game of tossing a coin. One person wins if heads comes up and the other person wins if it's tails. Let's look at how the three elements apply to this game.

1   *The balance of probability is even or 50–50.*

Tossing a coin is considered to be a fair game as both players have an equal chance of success. For every toss of the coin where heads wins there is an equal number of tosses where tails wins.

2   *The scale of payouts is typically one to one.*

Each player wagers the same amount of money as the other on each toss of the coin and the winner takes back their original wager, and the corresponding wager of the other player.

3   *The size of the positions, that is, the size of the wagers or bets.*

Typically, in a friendly game of coin toss both players will use the same size bet for every toss of the coin. This means that for each toss of the coin they will always wager a set amount of money, and not increase or decrease the size of the wager as the game progresses.

This innocent game of chance is often played by children who wager for marbles or some similarly innocuous commodity. If the game is played in the manner I have described, then the chances of winning or losing are equal and it is considered to be a fair game. If you play for long enough you should always break even and, ultimately, there should be no winners or losers. We will now look at how we can increase our chances of winning by managing the three elements of the game.

With regards to the first element, we cannot alter the probability of the outcomes so our chances of winning each toss of the coin will always be 50–50. However, if our opponent is silly enough we can set an uneven payout scale (the second element), where in the event we win our opponent pays us two marbles, and if we lose then we pay our opponent just one marble. But it is highly unlikely in a game of coin toss that our opponent would agree to such an unfair arrangement.

In fact, it is the last element that we can manage to our advantage. It is imperative that the size of our wager allows us to remain in the game long enough to win. If we are losing the game, then we can continue to play until we inevitably return to the break-even point. But the moment we are in front, we should quit the game. We may walk away with a black eye, as have many others when playing two-up, but we will be in profit. Figure 10.1 shows the balance of outcomes of tossing a coin 100 times.

Figure 10.1: balance of outcomes for 100 coin tosses

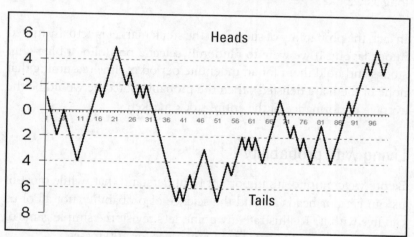

Over the course of our 100 tosses the balance of outcomes swung around the break-even point of zero. At different times in the process, the balance tipped in favour of either heads or tails. The balance of outcomes can temporarily deviate from zero but it will always return to this point of balance, provided the probability of outcomes is equal.

From this experiment, we can conclude that the balance of outcomes can, on average, be expected to deviate by four in either direction and can peak as high as seven during the course of 100 tosses. Using this information we can now establish a set of guidelines for managing the simple game of tossing a coin (please note that a sample of 100 tosses is inconclusive and has been used for illustrative purposes only):

- we must be prepared to play 100 times

- we must be able to sustain a maximum drawdown of seven losses

- we should quit the game as soon as we are winning by four tosses.

Tossing a coin, although a fair game of chance, can be managed to increase our probability of success. The risk of loss is virtually eradicated provided the probable outcome of a game is, at worst, break-even, and provided we can continue to play the game for as long as we like.

In fact, the probability of success in the stock market is actually tipped in our favour. If we were to randomly select a portfolio of blue-chip stocks and hold them for an indefinite period of time (assuming that none of them are delisted), then the probable outcome would be the average performance of the entire stock market.

Living with probability

Before we continue, it's important to understand that, while most of us can get our heads around the science of probability, not all of us can live with it. To illustrate my point, let's revisit the simple game of tossing a coin and the balance of outcomes for 100 tosses.

Now, while the probable outcome of tossing a coin is an even split between heads and tails, this doesn't mean that the outcome will oscillate perfectly between the two in a head, tail, head, tail pattern. As we have already discussed, it can in fact deviate by as much as seven, according to the above example, and it is this deviation that can be hard for us to tolerate.

Let's assume that you are betting on tails in our game of coin toss and you are therefore down by five tosses after the 21st game. In other words, you have lost 13 games and won only eight. But to make matters worse, let's assume that you aren't actually able to witness the tossing of the coin. Both players are simply being given the results of the game, played at another location, by a supposedly reliable third-party. Now ask yourself, if you were down 13 losses to eight wins, whether you would drop out of the game because you believed there was a bias in the process.

Let's also assume that the wager on each game is $1000. Now we have our heads telling us one thing, and our hip-pocket nerves telling us another. While we may understand the science of probability, many of us find it very hard to maintain our faith in it when the going gets tough.

A common expression of this phenomenon occurs when individuals can prove a strategy through comprehensive back-testing, only to dismiss it as a failure after trading it in real time for as little as 10 trades. Their ability to maintain their objectivity is lost in the face of mounting losses. Of course we all feel pain when we lose money, and this is why share trading isn't for everyone. It comes down to a question of faith in what we're doing—not just understanding.

Frame of reference

The average performance of a stock market over time is defined by the behaviour of its index, providing that the index in question is technically accurate. The All Ordinaries index represents approximately 90 per cent of the Australian stock market in terms of its market capitalisation and can be considered an accurate indicator of the overall market.

When tossing a coin, our frame of reference in terms of our probable success is 0 per cent. In the stock market, our frame of reference is the performance of the All Ordinaries index, which over the last century has risen approximately 9 per cent per annum. Of course, we have to be able to survive the odd bad year such as 1994 or 2002 (shown in figure 10.2, overleaf) when the market dropped over 10 per cent, as well as a really bad year such as 1987 or 2008 when the market crashed completely.

Figure 10.2: All Ordinaries index in 2002

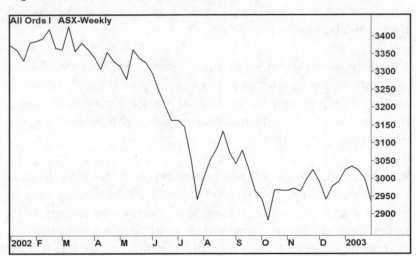

Therefore, when we evaluate the success or failure of our market strategy, we must benchmark it against 9 per cent per annum. If a market strategy is returning 9 per cent per annum, then it is performing no better than random share selection. If a strategy is returning *less* than 9 per cent per annum, then random share selection would actually be the superior method.

When evaluating someone else's strategy, such as that of a funds manager, it makes sense to compare it to the All Ordinaries. There is little sense in putting capital in a fund that outperforms the All Ordinaries by 2 per cent per annum when the annual administration fees are 2 per cent or more. My 12-year-old daughter could do just as good a job of investing money.

The law of averages

Given the good news that the market invariably rises over the long- term, it is astonishing that the majority of people who enter the stock market are not successful. The reason is the inability of most people to stay in the stock market long enough to exploit the law of averages. Basically, risk management is about surviving long enough to be able to apply the probable outcome of 9 per cent per annum as a frame of reference for our market strategy.

So by simply surviving in the stock market we can achieve a positive result, unlike the game of tossing a coin. In order to achieve this, we need to put an upper limit on the amount of money we are prepared to lose from each trade, thereby regulating the rate at which we deplete our total capital. Hence, the paradox—success in the stock market depends on how well you manage your losses, not your profits.

If you ask any experienced share trader, they'll tell you that even with a winning strategy it is quite common to suffer a string of up to eight consecutive losses. So hypothetically, if our total capital was $50 000 and we were to lose $5000 on eight consecutive occasions then our total capital would be reduced to $10 000 in a very short space of time. Not a very good survival strategy but an all too common story among investors who 'hung in there' throughout 2007 and 2008.

So to ensure long-term survival, we must regulate the size of our losses so that we can comfortably (read 'safely') sustain a string of repeated losses. We can achieve this by risking only a relatively small percentage of our total capital on each stock we buy.

For example, assume we have $50 000 total capital. On each new position we will risk only 10 per cent of our current total capital, as shown in table 10.1.

Table 10.1: 10 per cent risk on $50 000

Loss	Amount lost	Total remaining capital
1	$5000.00	$45 000.00
2	$4500.00	$40 500.00
3	$4050.00	$36 450.00
4	$3645.00	$32 805.00
5	$3280.50	$29 524.50
6	$2952.45	$26 572.05

Table 10.1 (*cont'd*): 10 per cent risk on $50 000

Loss	Amount lost	Total remaining capital
7	$2657.20	$23 914.84
8	$2391.48	$21 523.36

This method of regulating our losses gives us the ability to actually calculate the number of losses it would take for us be put out of the marketplace.

Let's assume that we're starting out with $50 000 total capital and once we have reached $5000 then we can no longer remain in the stock market. Figure 10.3 compares a 10 per cent loss per trade with a two per cent loss per trade.

Figure 10.3: 10 per cent loss versus 2 per cent loss

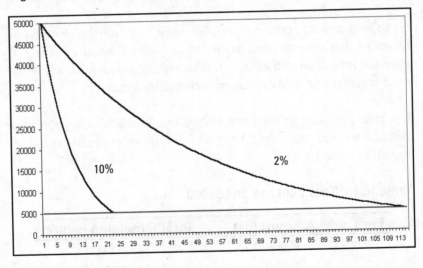

Three guesses as to which rule of thumb successful market participants employ. By using a 2 per cent risk rule we can sustain up to 115 consecutive losses, assuming we ignore the cost of brokerage. This is a reasonable assumption as our frame of reference of 9 per cent per annum, when applied to a capital base of $50 000, will more than offset our annual brokerage fees.

Using stop losses

To apply the concepts of risk management we must use stop losses. We cannot manage our losses unless we are prepared to sell shares that are falling in price. A common method employed by casual investors is to buy shares that are closer to their 52-week lows than they are to their 52-week highs. The idea behind this simple technique is that the shares carry less downside risk than they have upside potential.

Taken at face value, this method has merit. But most casual investors fail to employ this strategy properly because they don't have the discipline to sell the shares when their prices fall to their 52-week lows. By not selling at the 52-week lows, the investors who use this technique are not limiting their downside risk at all.

The toughest action any of us will ever have to take as market participants is to realise our losses. As already mentioned, it is the ability to take a loss that is the difference between success and failure in the stock market. Furthermore, it is only with a predetermined stop loss that we can calculate and manage risk. Here's an example:

- we have $50 000 total capital and are using the 2 per cent risk rule
- assume that our buy price of a share is $12 and we have set the stop loss price at $10
- therefore, the potential loss per share is $2 ($12 – $10)
- $1000 (2 per cent of $50 000) is the amount of money we are prepared to lose
- the number of shares we can buy is 500 ($1000 ÷ $2)
- the position size is $6000 (500 × $12)
- so, the percentage of total capital that can be spent on this position is 12 per cent ($6000 ÷ $50 000 × 100).

Therefore, to limit our risk to 2 per cent of total capital we must purchase no more than $6000 worth of shares (12 per cent of our total capital) and sell if the share price drops to $10. As active investors we have the advantage of having the range indicator, which gives us a predetermined stop loss price for performing our calculations. Using the chart of company J, shown in figure 10.4 we will do the calculations using actual figures from the range indicator.

Figure 10.4: company J share price chart showing the range indicator

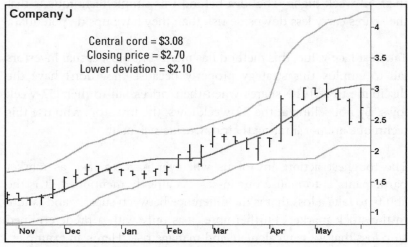

Looking at the right-hand edge of the chart we can see that the price activity has fallen into the buy zone and then closed up for one week, indicating the presence of buyer support. The green light is flashing for an entry and it's time to do our risk management. However, there are a couple of problems with using the closing price as our entry price in the calculations.

The first problem is that the share price could move higher when the stock market opens on Monday morning. We would then be forced to re-do our risk management calculations during the trading day. The second problem is that we have not allowed for brokerage fees. So a quick and easy solution to both of these problems is to use the value of the central cord rather than the closing price when doing our sums. Here's an example of how to calculate our position size:

- we have $50 000 total capital and are using the 2 per cent risk rule

- the central cord price is $3.08 and the lower deviation is $2.10

- therefore, the potential loss per share is $0.98 ($3.08 − $2.10)
- $1000 is the amount of money we are prepared to lose (2 per cent of $50 000)
- the number of shares we can buy is 1020 ($1000 ÷ $0.98)
- the position size is $3142 (1020 × $3.08)
- so, the percentage of total capital that can be spent on this position is 6.3 per cent ($3142 ÷ $50 000 × 100).

On Monday morning I will ring my stockbroker and issue instructions, saying I want to purchase $3142 worth of company J shares, and that I will pay up to $3.08 per share. It's his job to work out the number of shares that need to be purchased and my job to monitor the stop loss on a weekly basis. In my weekly newsletter I publish the two per cent risk rule calculations for all the shares listed and give the percentage of total capital that can be spent on each position.

Sector risk

The type of risk we have looked at so far is referred to as position risk. We now need to consider other forms of risk that we will be exposed to in the stock market. In the early part of the new millennium, resource and energy stocks dominated the landscape. So our dynamic analysis was looking somewhat lopsided, in favour of the multitude of resource and energy stocks that were trending up as a result of this popularity.

Our 'fundamentals' filter was doing a good job of keeping out many undesirables, but the prices of any fundamentally sound blue-chip stocks that were even remotely connected to commodities or energy were trending up. These shares were rising in price largely because of the industrialisation of mainland China and its impact on commodity prices, as opposed to any other factors.

While these shares qualified as potential trading opportunities, investing in them meant exposure to a sector that was being driven up predominantly by speculation. We must limit our exposure to the risk of speculation in any sector that becomes overly fashionable, with respect to both our total capital and the number of individual positions. The following example explains why:

- we have $50 000 total capital and limit our sector risk to 30 per cent of total capital
- assume that we will spread 30 per cent of $50 000 ($15 000) across six positions
- our position risk is 2 per cent per share, which makes our total position risk per sector 12 per cent
- the sector collapses and we sell all six positions when they reach their stop losses
- we have lost a total of 12 per cent of our total capital, which equals $6000.

So while we have limited our exposure to each sector to just 30 per cent of our total capital, we have still suffered a total loss of 12 per cent. This is because we have a concentration of individual positions in one particular sector, a situation that we must be mindful to avoid. The maximum amount of total capital that I allocate per sector is 30 per cent, while I also limit my total position risk per sector to 6 per cent, which equates to a maximum of three positions.

Portfolio and specific equity risk

Portfolio risk is the danger we face from our own market strategy and our mistakes in implementing it. Part of the process of dynamic analysis is the qualitative assessment of MMA charts. It would be presumptuous to assume that our judgement of these charts is always correct. We are also relying on the research and opinions of others when it comes to finding shares with good fundamentals and, from time to time, we may find that this faith is misplaced.

Our market strategy is designed to shift the balance of probability in our favour as opposed to being the perfect answer to buying and selling shares. Unless we are prepared to pay for arrogance in hard currency, we need to limit our exposure to our own fallibility. Portfolio or system risk is the sum total of our position risk and it is calculated by multiplying the number of positions we own by our individual position risk, that is, 2 per cent of total capital.

For example, if we are using the 2 per cent risk rule and we have seven different positions in our portfolio, then portfolio risk or total market exposure is 2 per cent multiplied by seven, or 14 per cent. In the event that our trading strategy is systemically flawed or a stock market crash occurs, our maximum exposure is only 14 per cent of total capital. So in a similar vein to limiting our risk per sector, we must also limit our total portfolio risk. To do this, we must establish guidelines to govern the maximum number of positions we have in our portfolio, as follows:

- our total portfolio risk should not exceed 20 per cent of total capital
- therefore, using 2 per cent position risk we can own a maximum of 10 positions.

But, there's a flipside to this where we must also limit the minimum number of stocks we own and the maximum amount of capital we allocate to each. This is because we must also take into consideration specific equity risk, which is the risk associated with each stock or company.

A good example would be where a company suffers a major product recall, causing its share price to instantly collapse. The share price will crash through your stop loss and your only protection would be to limit your total exposure to each position. If we take into account equity risk as well as portfolio risk, then we come up with the following combined guidelines:

- our total portfolio risk cannot exceed 20 per cent of total capital
- therefore, using 2 per cent position risk we can own a maximum of 10 positions
- no single position can be greater than 20 per cent of our total capital
- therefore, we can own a minimum of five positions.

Note that the more positions we have, the higher our portfolio risk. Therefore, we generally want to minimise the number of positions we have in our portfolio. But there is a lower limit as well because we don't want to overly expose ourselves to specific equity risk. Like most things in life, it's a balancing act between two extremes.

Why 2 per cent is optimal

Several key points are now worth mentioning. Firstly, 2 per cent is optimal. In other words, don't try to go one better by using a 1 per cent risk rule. If you risk 2 per cent per trade then your portfolio will end up having about eight to 10 individual positions, as each position size will be between 10 and 12 per cent of your total capital. Using a 1 per cent risk rule will result in approximately twice this number of positions which will conflict with our portfolio risk guideline of having a maximum of 10.

Furthermore, if you risk only 1 per cent of total capital on each position, then you end up diluting your overall performance. If we diversify our portfolio unnecessarily we will be doing ourselves more harm than good. The rate of return pyramid shown in figure 10.5 shows that there are only a small number of stocks that give the highest possible rate of return.

Figure 10.5: rate of return pyramid

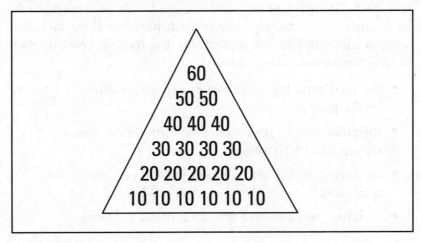

60
50 50
40 40 40
30 30 30 30
20 20 20 20 20
10 10 10 10 10 10

As you can see, there are very few stocks with a high rate of return of 60 per cent, while there are a lot of stocks with only a 10 per cent rate of return.

If you only own five stocks, then you can optimise the average performance of your portfolio by having most, if not all, of your holdings near the top of the pyramid. But if you diversify unnecessarily, then you will be forced to own stocks that have a lower rate of return. What's more, the situation would be further exacerbated during tough times when there are even fewer good stocks to choose from. So, using diversification as a form of risk management is very much a double-edged sword.

Risk management and gearing

This is where implementing sound quantitative risk management becomes critical. In order to sensibly utilise gearing, we need to start by breaking down our total capital into low, medium, and high risk segments that can then be managed separately. A prudent capital allocation would be:

40% of total capital	→	Low risk — income portfolio of asset class shares
40% of total capital	→	Medium risk — an actively managed share portfolio
20% of total capital	→	High risk — high leverage derivatives such as CFDs

As a leverage instrument, I like CFDs because they provide up to 10:1 gearing and aren't subject to time decay like warrants and options. However, like most products that offer leverage, they are often traded with scant regard for their magnified downside risk. Novice traders will often fall for the trap of trading their equity rather than trading the behavioural nature of the underlying financial instrument. It is very foolhardy to try to trade BHP with 10:1 gearing as it is equivalent to a 10 per cent drawdown, as shown in figure 10.6 (overleaf). If you try to maintain your gearing at a ratio of 10:1 by constantly increasing your position size, then it is highly likely that you will be prematurely stopped out of BHP by a margin call.

Figure 10.6: trading BHP with 10:1 gearing

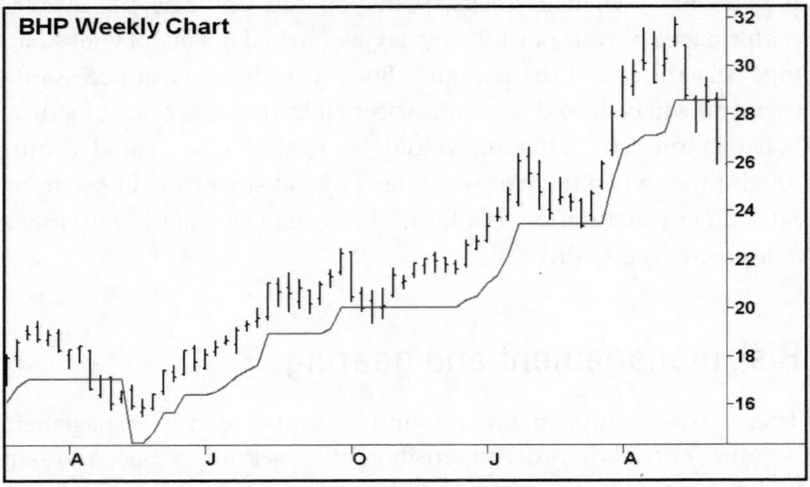

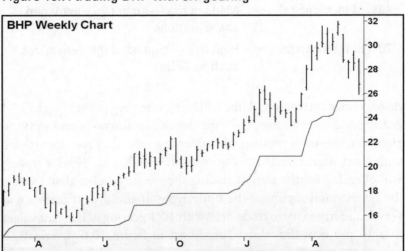

A far more realistic (read 'sustainable') gearing ratio for trading BHP would be 5:1, which translates into a 20 per cent drawdown, shown in figure 10.7.

Figure 10.7: trading BHP with 5:1 gearing

We can cross-correlate different gearing levels with their corresponding volatility levels, as follows:

10:1 gearing	→	10% drawdown
8:1 gearing	→	13% drawdown
6:1 gearing	→	17% drawdown
5:1 gearing	→	20% drawdown
4:1 gearing	→	25% drawdown
3:1 gearing	→	33% drawdown

The gearing ratio for a CFD trade isn't determined by what the CFD provider is willing to offer in terms of leverage, but by what the underlying financial instrument will tolerate in terms of volatility. In the case of RIO Tinto Limited (see figure 10.8), we can just get away with 7:1 gearing, or a 15 per cent drawdown.

Figure 10.8: trading RIO with 7:1 gearing

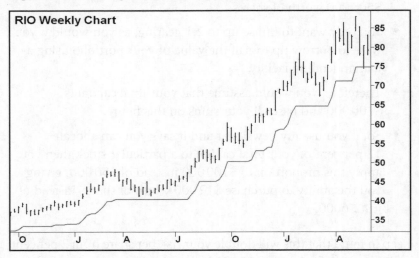

In fact, if a stock like RIO can tolerate a 15 per cent drawdown then I would actually recommend that you trade it using a gearing level *lower* than that which matches the drawdown level you would use as the stop loss. In the previous example of RIO, I would trade it with a drawdown stop loss of 15 per cent but use no more than 5:1 gearing.

Of course, even 5:1 gearing is fairly aggressive and it won't take too many losses with this level of gearing to blow your entire high risk capital allocation. But that's why they call it high risk and why we allocate only 20 per cent of our total capital to it in the first place.

Using CFDs with the active investing strategy

For those who find the previous explanation of how CFDs work to be a bit confusing, here's an alternative way of approaching the subject—treat CFDs as if they were a margin loan. This is also a far less aggressive way of employing CFDs, and a way that they can be used in conjunction with the active investing strategy. The best way of explaining this approach is with a working example. Let's assume you have $50 000 total capital to trade with and you open a CFD account:

- For all the leading blue-chip stocks you will be provided with up to 10:1 gearing, giving you the ability to control up to $500 000 worth of shares.

- You only want to utilise up to 2:1 gearing, as you would if you were to borrow up to half the value of your portfolio using a margin lending facility.

- Therefore, you would assume that your total capital is $100 000 and base all your sums on this figure.

- So, if you use my newsletter and it says you can allocate 12 per cent of your total capital to a particular stock then you apply this proportion to $100 000 instead of $50 000, giving you the ability to purchase $12 000 worth of shares instead of just $6000.

Keep in mind that this will double your risk per share from 2 per cent to 4 per cent of your own $50 000, so you still need to break down your total capital into different risk segments where this would be considered at least a medium-risk strategy. Also note that the CFD provider is charging interest on the entire value of your holdings and not just the half that you're borrowing, as would be the case with a margin loan.

Conduct regular performance reviews

It is essential to understand that no amount of risk management will turn a losing strategy into a winning one. If a market strategy consistently loses money over time then risk management will only prolong the agony.

We must constantly test and measure our market performance to ensure that our market strategy is working for us and not against us. In the case of active investing, I consider it prudent to analyse my performance on a half-yearly to yearly basis. Analysing my returns in a shorter timeframe is unrealistic given the nature of blue-chip stocks. On the other hand, checking over a longer timeframe could be costly if market conditions change and I don't adapt accordingly.

Asset allocation

Although I'm mentioning it last, asset allocation is probably one of the most critical areas when it comes to preserving your wealth. This is an exercise that I feel everyone should perform on an annual basis at least, and one that becomes far more critical as we approach retirement. This is because an imbalance in our asset allocation can expose us to the totally unnecessary risk of a catastrophic event occurring within a single asset class. So, let's assume you have your money spread across the following asset classes:

Figure 10.9: asset allocation

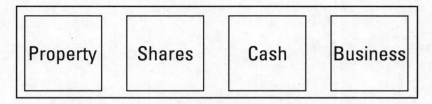

A sensible set of guidelines for the average investor would be:

- have enough cash to live on for two years in case your investments stop producing sufficient income

- the value of your shares should not exceed the value of your property assets

- retain your business interests if possible, for example, become a silent partner

- make sure your assets are legally protected

- establish financial structures to minimise tax.

Where possible, I believe it's a good idea to retain your business interests into retirement, as this is a good hedge for times when both property and stock market assets dip simultaneously. While this scenario is exceptionally unlikely, as they are normally counter-cyclical asset classes, having the entire global banking system almost come to a complete standstill in 2008 also looked exceptionally unlikely until it actually happened.

Chapter 11

Factors that affect opinion

The US sneezes and we all catch a cold

Our sole purpose in applying dynamic analysis so far has been to locate and exploit the impact of fundamentals as a factor that affects opinion. We have verified the presence of sound fundamentals and then tested and measured their effect on share price activity. In doing so, we have eliminated the need to *wait* for prices to rise, which so many passive investors and fundamentalists think of as a hallmark of successful investing. This may explain the absence of youth in this group of investors.

The significance of dynamic analysis however, is far wider reaching than this single application. We will now look again at the major factors that affect opinion in table 11.1 (overleaf), and expand on their properties with respect to their timeframe and degree of predictability. As active investors, we are working with weekly charts in a medium-term timeframe, so the prioritisation of the list is based on this aspect of our market strategy. If we were monitoring share prices on a daily basis and wanting to be in and out of the market quickly, then the structure of our list would change dramatically, with fundamentals probably appearing at the bottom.

Table 11.1: factors that affect opinion

Factor	Timeframe	Predictability
Fundamentals	Medium-term	Good
Global factors	Medium-term	Good
Macro economics	Medium-term	Good
Market cycles	Long-term	Fair
News and rumours	Short-term	Poor
Gambling and speculation	Short-term	Poor

We would also be preoccupied with monitoring daily news and company announcements as these factors would have a large impact within our timeframe. The purpose of prioritising the list in the first place is so that we can focus our limited resources as small business owners as efficiently as possible. Now that we've prioritised our list we must look at how we can test and measure each factor.

Fundamentals

This factor is first on our list and one of the cornerstones of active investing. Its importance can never be underestimated. It is the main driving force behind most of the money in stock markets around the world, and has been the number-one long-term influence on share prices since the inception of equity markets.

We could achieve a positive result by simply testing and measuring this factor alone. All other factors affecting opinion take a back seat to a company's fundamentals when it comes to movements in its share price over the long-term.

Global factors

Global factors include any phenomenon that occurs in offshore markets that will have an impact on the Australian stock market.

There is very clear historical evidence to support the fact that the ebbs and flows of our stock market closely mirror those of our neighbour on the other side of the Pacific. Hence the saying, the US sneezes and Australia catches a cold. We are also influenced by the wellbeing or otherwise of Asian markets. This is because companies in the Asia–Pacific region are the primary customers for most of the commodities produced in Australia. For example, the run-up in our resources sector in recent times was fuelled by the industrialisation of mainland China.

Probably the least influential offshore markets are the European bourses, which include England, France and Germany, among others. So when it comes to global or broad market influences, the US is number one in the eyes of most Australian investors, be they individuals or institutions.

It is a rare occurrence for us to enjoy a sustained uptrend when US markets are in decline and we inevitably follow their lead when it comes to stock market crashes. Their influence emanates mainly from the New York Stock Exchange, which is considered by most investors as the centre of the universe. The NASDAQ market is made up of predominantly technology stocks and is of far less significance.

Table 11.2 shows the three main US indices, along with the relevant exchange, the number of companies they represent and their proportion of market capitalisation.

Table 11.2: main US indices

Index	Market	No. of companies	Market capitalisation
Dow Jones Industrial Average	NYSE	30	20%
Standard & Poors 500 Index	NYSE & NASDAQ	500	N/A
NASDAQ Composite	NASDAQ	5000	100%

When the US markets are trending down, the rest of the world usually follows in sympathy. The reasoning behind a broad market downtrend doesn't alter the impact it has on the Australian market — we inevitably follow suit.

For example, in early 2001 the Japanese Government forced many Japanese banks to foreclose on bad debts. The banks could no longer list these debts on their balance sheets, and a day *We can test* of reckoning for many Japanese financial institutions was *and measure* fast approaching. This had a massive flow-on effect in the *the broad* US which, at the time, was the largest offshore lender to *market using* Japan. The US markets became very nervous and fell for *index charts.* several trading days. The Australian stock market in turn, and for no logical reason, fell in sympathy with their US counterparts. We had little to no exposure to the Japanese banks but this was irrelevant in the face of falling US markets.

Crossover charts

As you can see, the behaviour of the broad market, predominately the US, can overtake other factors that drive Australian share prices. There are many rational thinkers who would debate the logic behind this phenomenon but as active investors we are concerned with the practicalities of the market, rather than comprehending its governing logic, or lack thereof.

We can test and measure the broad market using index charts. The charts in figure 11.1 show the S&P 500 index from the US and our All Ordinaries index. These are daily charts and they include a 10-day exponential moving average (grey line) and a 30-day exponential moving average (black line). As we have done with the MMA charts, the price activity has been switched off because we are only interested in the moving averages.

The 10-day exponential moving average (EMA) is referred to as a fast-moving average and it tracks the index more closely than the 30-day EMA, which is called a slow-moving average. When the fast-moving average is below the slow-moving average the index is in retreat and heading downwards. When the fast EMA is above the slow EMA the index is trending upwards.

Figure 11.1: S&P 500 and All Ords EMA charts

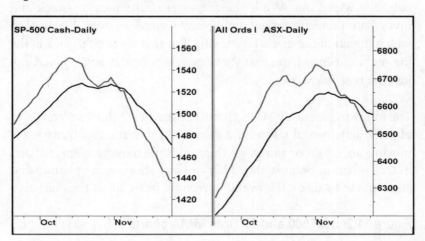

These charts are referred to as 'crossover' charts. We use them to answer the simple question of whether or not the indices are trending up or down. They are simple in construction and provide us with robust and unambiguous signals.

A broad market decline is signalled when both the indices are retreating at the same time. While we don't want to overreact to a broad market decline by proactively selling shares, it is not a time to be opening new positions. To build this action into our strategy we have to add the following instruction to our space monkey's rule book:

> **Do not open new positions when both crossover charts are crossed to the downside.**

This tells us when to leave our money in the bank and stand aside. If we can see from the crossover charts that the broad market is in decline, then it pays to wait until the market has turned up again before opening new positions. The crossover charts act as a safety net, alerting us when we're no longer in sync with the broad market.

The long-term trend

If we try to swim against the direction of the broad market then at best we will be wasting our time and at worst we will be slowly and painfully wiped out. While the crossover charts provide quick and immediate protection, they don't really give us an overall view of in which direction the market is moving. For that we need to look at the big picture using charts that show us years of price activity, and not just the past few weeks.

The following monthly MMA charts in figure 11.2 show several years of price activity and tell us at a glance whether the broad market is moving up, down or sideways. I use multiple moving average charts in this situation because they filter out any short-term volatility and allow me to focus on the overall direction, or trend, of the markets.

Figure 11.2: S&P 500 and All Ords MMA charts

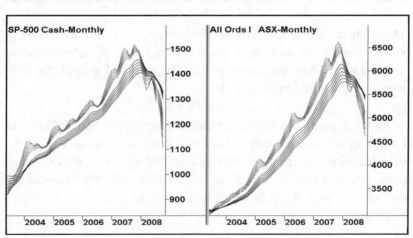

From figure 11.2 we can see that once the broad market had topped out at the end of October 2007 it was all downhill. So, we would have refrained from purchasing any new shares from this point on as we would have been trading counter to the trend of the broad market and throwing good money after bad. In this way, the crossover charts and long-term charts work together to provide us with a complete solution for dealing with the markets from an overall perspective.

Macro economics

When Alan Greenspan was Chairman of the US Federal Reserve, he was referred to as 'God' by many investors because of the Federal Reserve's ability to influence the direction of world equity markets. His address to the US Congress in October 2000 demonstrated this power. During the address, Greenspan indicated that he was concerned with the heightened sense of wealth that stock ownership was having on consumers, and its flow-on effect on inflation. In the 24 hours that followed this address, global equity markets fell by an average of three per cent. Events such as this are completely unpredictable, and therefore make short-term speculators very nervous.

Greenspan was well aware of the power his words carried, and he used them very effectively to control speculative activity in the marketplace. Those who disapprove of this form of crowd control should revisit history and note the Federal Reserve's complete ineffectiveness in the lead-up to the great crash of 1929.

On a more significant level, the US Federal Reserve can indirectly regulate equity markets by either tightening or easing money supply to the markets via official interest rates. The following chart of the Dow Jones Industrial Average (figure 11.3) shows the effect of an interest rate tightening cycle that began in 1999.

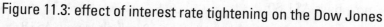

Figure 11.3: effect of interest rate tightening on the Dow Jones

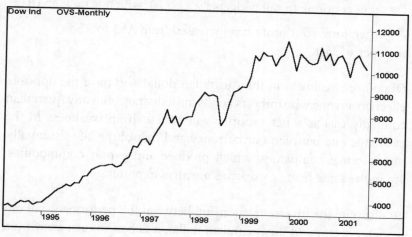

The chart shows with great clarity how, on this particular occasion, the tightening of interest rates had an immediate impact on equity markets. Therefore, it is conventional doctrine that the raising of interest rates will have a negative effect on the price of equities, as dividend yields tend to move with official interest rates. However, it is the timing of the flow-on effect that has everyone stumped — including the US Federal Reserve.

The good news is that in the event of a significant decline in world equity markets the crossover charts will inevitably cross to the downside, protecting us against any negative influence from macro economic factors. Furthermore, we can actually exploit the more subtle impact macro economic factors can have on individual market sectors to our advantage. What's more, to do this we don't need to have an intimate understanding of these economic factors or how they affect certain industries. To demonstrate how we are going to test and measure the effect of these factors we will look at a specific example. Imagine you are an Australian manufacturer exporting widgets to the U.S, and:

- each widget costs you A$10 to produce
- US$1.00 is equivalent to A$1.50
- you sell your widgets for US$10, which is A$15
- the Australian dollar falls against the US dollar and US$1.00 now buys A$1.80
- you continue to sell widgets for US$10, which is now A$18
- therefore, your profit has increased from A$5 to A$8 per widget.

Of course, weakness in the Australian dollar will have the opposite effect on anyone who imports goods into Australia. But any Australian company that is a net exporter will benefit from weakness in the exchange rate between our currency and that of the US. Essentially, our resource companies, which produce and export commodities, are in the same boat as we are as a widget exporter.

To illustrate the inverse relationship between the performance of our resource sector and the Australian dollar, it is best to turn away from recent events and go back to a time when there were far fewer factors affecting this sector. Very early in the new millennium was such a time, and figures 11.4 and 11.5 allow you to compare the overall trend in our resource sector with the exchange rate at the time. In order to observe our resource sector as a whole at this point, it is best to use the now discontinued All Resources index.

Figure 11.4: All Resources index chart

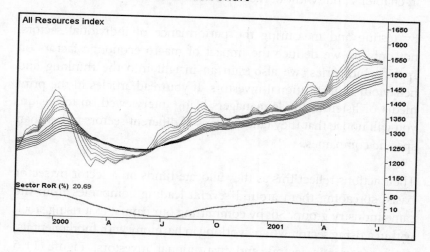

Figure 11.5: value of the Australian dollar vs. the US dollar

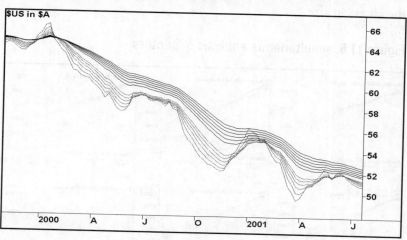

As one chart goes up the other comes down, graphically demonstrating their inverse relationship. Once again I have employed MMA charts because I am interested in the overall trend of each sector and I don't want to be distracted by any short-term volatility. I have also applied a sector rate of return indicator because we can measure and compare the profitability of individual sectors in exactly the same way as we do with stocks. This indicator is identical to the one described in chapter 7, but without the horizontal lines at 20 and 30 per cent.

By testing and measuring the performance of individual sectors, not only do we deduce the impact of macro economic factors on specific industries, we also gain an insight into the thinking and behaviour of institutional investors. If you read articles in the print media or listen to funds managers being interviewed on television, you will notice that they talk in terms of different sectors rather than specific companies.

Their actions reflect this as they allocate funds on a sector by sector basis, spreading them around several leading companies from the same industry group. So, by committing our capital to a rising stock within a rising sector, we are working in harmony with fundamentals, macro economic factors and institutional investors. Figure 11.6 shows how we can assess several sectors at the same time by reducing the charts in size.

Figure 11.6: simultaneous analysis of sectors

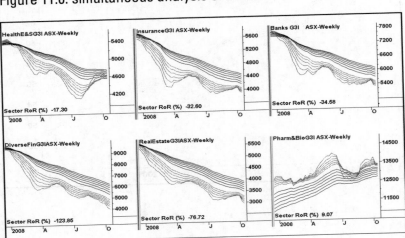

I believe that the importance of sector analysis is secondary to that of an individual company's fundamentals and, therefore, my preferred approach is to use sector charts to overcome any indecision. For instance, if I have two stocks, both with acceptable MMA charts and similar rates of return, then the stock from the best performing sector would be my first choice.

We can certainly see from the above sector charts that things looked very bleak in late 2008. By periodically checking these charts I carry in the back of my mind a general picture of which sectors are doing what. This picture then influences my share selection, on an almost subconscious level. However, it is important to remember that sector picking is secondary to our primary strategy of selecting individual stocks using dynamic analysis.

Market cycles

The presence of timing cycles in the stock market is a well-established fact and we have already seen evidence of them in chapter 5. However, there are also much longer term market cycles and phases that it pays to be mindful of. Over the past quarter of a century, our market has passed through two bullish and one non-bullish period as shown in figure 11.7.

Figure 11.7: bullish and non-bullish periods in the All Ordinaries

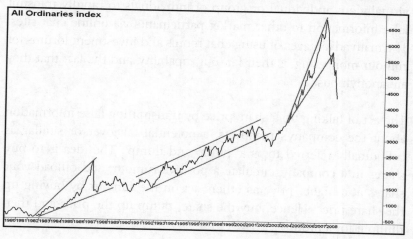

The market has a strong tendency to alternate between bullish and non-bullish phases because, having just witnessed a boom–bust cycle, investors become very conservative in their behaviour and as a result the market settles down into a period of far more subdued growth. These non-bullish phases, which are identified on a chart using two parallel lines, generally last for very long periods, such as the one seen during the 1990s.

Active investing is well suited to these times as it relies on the market being driven by rational forces such as fundamentals, which usually results in reduced volatility. Given that we have recently witnessed a bullish phase, it is very likely that we will now experience a sustained period of relatively subdued growth on the back of it, and this bodes well for the active investing strategy.

News and rumours

News and rumours generally have an unpredictable and short-term effect on price behaviour. There is, however, a deliberate attempt by some market participants to use the influence of these factors to gain an advantage in the marketplace. While some rumours are true, there are many that are falsely created to temporarily shift share prices in a predetermined direction.

Technology has lent a hand in circulating rumours by allowing virtually any individual or group of individuals to rapidly transmit false information to other market participants via online chat sites. The main advantages of using chat rooms and investment forums for rumour mongering, is their fan-out capability, and the fact that they are anonymous.

The act of talking up a share price by transmitting false information about the company's prospects, a potential takeover or similar, is colloquially referred to as a 'pump and dump'. The idea is to buy shares in a company, circulate a positive rumour, and offload your shares at a higher price as others act on the rumour by buying up the share price. Hence, buy the share, pump up the price and then dump it for a profit.

However, some rumours are true and to act on them can generate handsome returns in a very short space of time. This leads many market participants into the trap of acting on unsubstantiated tips and rumours. What's more, the spreading of rumours is not limited to the internet. Many stockbrokers use access to rumours as a marketing hook, refering to it as the 'word on the street'.

Luckily, as active investors we are working in a timeframe that is relatively immune to the short-term impact of announcements and rumours. Therefore, I pay scant attention to them, and would suggest that trading or investing on this basis be considered little more than a form of gambling.

Gambling and speculation

Speaking of gambling, another side-effect of technology is the high level of accessibility we all have to the stock market. Online broking means we can instantly buy and sell shares from the comfort of our own home at discount brokerage rates, which are comparable in magnitude to the price of a cinema ticket.

This level of accessibility has opened the doors to the stock market being treated as a type of virtual casino. Fortunately, the influence of speculators who drive and feed off the rumour mill and individuals who gamble and punt on share price movements is minimal.

Keep it simple

No doubt we could actively search for other factors that affect opinion and ways to test and measure their influence. But we have now reached the point where, given our limited personal resources, we would be deviating from our original objectives. We would be putting in too much time and effort for minimal improvements in our returns.

By testing and measuring every fundamentally sound blue-chip stock for a rising share price, we are performing what traders refer to as 'bottom-up' analysis—a task that would have been beyond contemplation several decades ago, prior to the advent of personal computing.

We are also performing 'top-down' analysis, by showing a preference for stocks in rising sectors. We are constantly monitoring the broad market conditions and taking into account the long-term market cycles. Our overall strategy as active investors is comprehensive in design, and highly efficient in its use of our time. To go beyond our current level of refinement is to entertain unnecessary complexity. The best way to turn a good trading system into a bad trading system is to try and make it a perfect system.

Chapter 12

How does it all work?

See how active investing works in real time

This chapter is written by Simon Sherwood.

Now that we know all the theory behind the active investing strategy and what it takes to be an active investor, it's time to see how it all works in real time. Well, in the time it takes to read this chapter!

For this real-life simulation, we are going to be using the ActVest newsletter, which provides all the information required to correctly implement the active investing strategy. Also, to track our portfolio we will use the ActVest trade recorder, which is an easy-to-use Excel spreadsheet. It contains a few useful tools that will simplify our buying and selling calculations. These are the only tools we will be using during the simulation, and we will be going through the same procedure used in the active investing workshops. Here's an outline of the process we will be following:

- check the stop losses for all our open positions
- check the crossover charts to see if we can enter the market
- select suitable MMA charts

- check the stocks in data tables to see if we have a valid entry
- work out the purchase details, that is, our position size
- update our records.

We will be doing this over the period of one month, which will give you a clearer indication as to how the system works and how much time and effort is involved in being an active investor. For the sake of this simulation we will only be using data from the ActVest newsletter for our entry calculations. We've chosen the month of April 2007, so enough time has lapsed since then that there's no chance of any of the stocks we select being interpreted as current recommendations.

Week one

We're starting with $100 000 cash, and for this simulation we'll ignore brokerage costs and dividends (dividends are usually much greater than brokerage costs). Figure 12.1 shows a picture of the ActVest trade recorder. You can see that our 'cash on hand' is $100 000 and our 'total capital' (the value of our shares plus cash on hand) is also $100 000. When we do a transaction we'll enter the newsletter name in the form NLYYMMDD (for the week ending 6 April 2007, it would be NL070406) into the 'newsletter' field. The spreadsheet will then be saved under that file name when we click the 'new week' button.

Figure 12.1: ActVest trade recorder

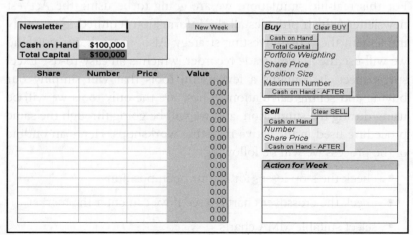

The first thing we will do is check the long-term MMA and crossover charts of the S&P 500 and All Ordinaries (see figures 12.2 and 12.3).

Figure 12.2: long-term MMA charts for S&P 500 and All Ords

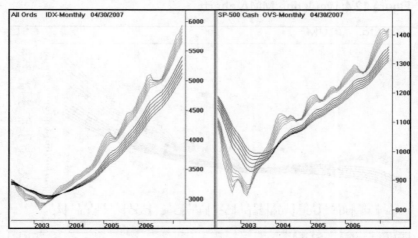

Figure 12.3: crossover charts for S&P 500 and All Ords

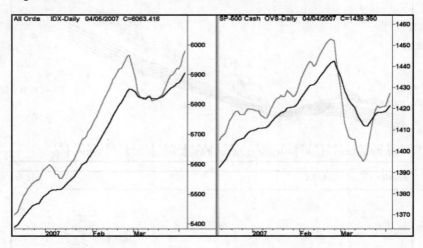

Based on the long-term trends, we can see that this is an appropriate time to be buying shares. The crossover charts are also both crossed to the upside, which gives us a green light for this particular week.

It's now time to examine the MMA charts. For this week there were nine pages in total, showing about 68 stocks. Having looked over them, my list of prospects is CSL, FKP, Melbourne IT (MLB), OneSteel (OST) and The Reject Shop (TRS). Their MMA charts can be seen in figure 12.4.

Figure 12.4: week one MMA charts

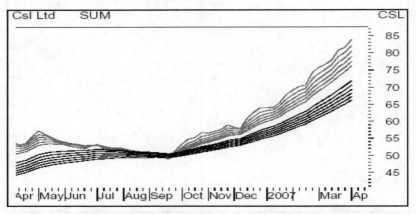

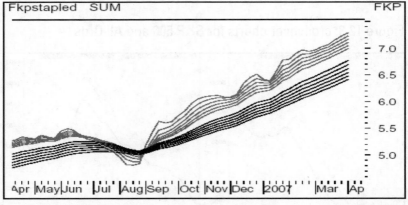

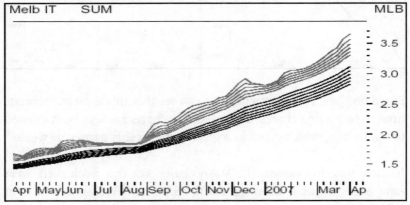

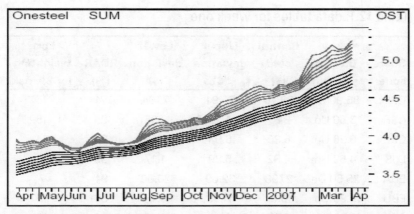

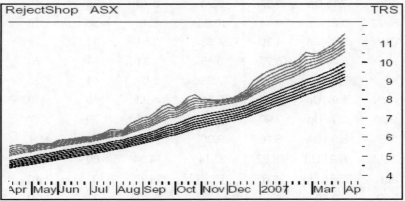

Now it's time to see if there are any valid entries. To do this, we'll look at an extract from the data tables in table 12.1 (overleaf). The data tables provide all the figures we need to work out if a stock is in the buy zone. We can also work out the position size using the 'portfolio weighting' value.

For a valid entry, the closing price must be between the value of the central cord and the lower deviation (as explained in chapter 9). It also must be an up week, that is, the week's closing price must be greater than that of the previous week. Lastly, the rate of return (shown as ROAR in the data tables) must be equal to or greater than 30 per cent. Based on these conditions, we can see that all the stocks we have selected, with the exception of MLB, meet these criteria.

Table 12.1: data tables for week one

Share code	Closing price ($)	Central cord ($)	Upper deviation ($)	Lower deviation ($)	ROAR (%)	Port. weighting for 2% risk
CSL	85.90 Up	88.70	95.91	77.04	74	15
CSR	3.56 Up	3.87	4.23	3.35	25	15
CXP	6.30 Up	6.38	6.93	5.50	24	14
DJS	4.59 Up	4.92	5.39	4.17	55	13
ERA	25.50 Dn	27.98	32.69	20.60	91	7
FBU	9.99 Up	10.62	11.53	9.18	36	14
FKP	7.35 Up	7.57	8.24	6.48	39	13
FWD	9.02 Up	9.41	10.00	8.45	56	19
GWT	3.99 Dn	4.20	4.63	3.51	31	12
HIL	5.44 Dn	5.77	6.15	5.31	34	20
HPX	2.00 Up	2.018	2.36	2.07	44	20
HVN	4.92 Up	5.06	5.51	4.33	49	13
HWI	2.74 Up	2.90	3.26	2.31	79	9
IRE	8.00 Dn	8.16	9.00	6.79	31	11
JBM	17.92 Up	18.62	21.14	14.54	60	9
LEI	35.55 Up	38.67	43.25	31.25	92	10
LEP	3.90	4.40	4.74	4.02	21	20
MBL	84.50 Up	87.53	93.09	79.38	30	20
MCR	3.21 Up	3.52	4.25	2.33	110	5
MFS	5.33 Up	5.83	6.45	5.05	59	14
MGR	5.55 Up	5.96	6.45	5.27	26	17
MLB	3.72	3.79	4.16	3.20	63	12
MND	11.35 Up	11.80	13.15	9.63	90	10
MOC	3.15 Up	3.09	3.30	2.75	30	18
MRE	8.12 Up	7.83	9.20	5.62	57	7
MTS	5.02 Up	5.04	5.44	4.39	27	15
MXG	4.52 Up	4.80	5.27	4.12	46	14
NWS	30.36 Dn	31.97	33.78	30.37	21	20
ORG	8.74 Dn	9.72	10.53	8.55	48	16
OST	5.36 Up	5.47	5.87	4.82	42	16
PRG	5.30 Up	5.52	5.95	4.85	33	16

Share code	Closing price ($)	Central cord ($)	Upper deviation ($)	Lower deviation ($)	ROAR (%)	Port. weighting for 2% risk
QAN	5.25	5.89	6.27	5.27	44	19
QBE	32.15 Up	33.84	36.41	29.68	56	16
RIN	18.48 Up	20.48	21.78	18.42	27	19
RUP	13.85 Up	14.20	14.89	13.15	25	20
SBC	16.95 Up	17.88	19.18	15.77	20	16
SDG	3.28 Dn	4.11	4.65	3.48	52	13
SEK	7.30 Up	8.16	9.01	6.83	80	12
SEV	11.42	12.23	13.27	10.72	36	16
SGP	8.58 Up	8.89	9.55	8.09	25	20
SGT	2.75 Up	3.01	3.31	2.65	45	17
SLM	4.00	4.32	4.66	3.76	41	15
TLS	4.69 Up	4.69	5.04	4.13	37	16
TRG	13.69 Up	15.11	16.97	13.95	23	20
TRS	11.88 Up	12.01	13.14	10.20	70	13

Now it's time to work out how much of each stock we can buy—our position size. We will use the 'buy calculator' section of the ActVest trade recorder to help us out (see figure 12.5). By clicking on the cash on hand and total capital buttons, the respective amounts are transferred across. I've entered in the portfolio weighting (from the data tables) and also the share price of CSL, which is $85.

Figure 12.5: the buy calculator for CSL in week one

Buy	Clear BUY	
Cash on Hand		100,000
Total Capital		100,000
Portfolio Weighting		15
Share Price		85
Position Size		**15,000**
Maximum Number		**176**
Cash on Hand – AFTER		**85,040**

The buy calculator has worked out that our position size for CSL is \$15000 and that therefore, at the current price, we can buy 176 shares.

I'll enter the details for CSL into the trade recorder, update the cash on hand field, clear the buy calculator and finally, make a note about the purchase. Also, because we are now doing a transaction, I'll enter the newsletter reference. This process then needs to be repeated for the remaining stocks—FKP, OST and TRS. This is what our portfolio will look like at the end of the first week:

Figure 12.6: trade recorder at the end of week one

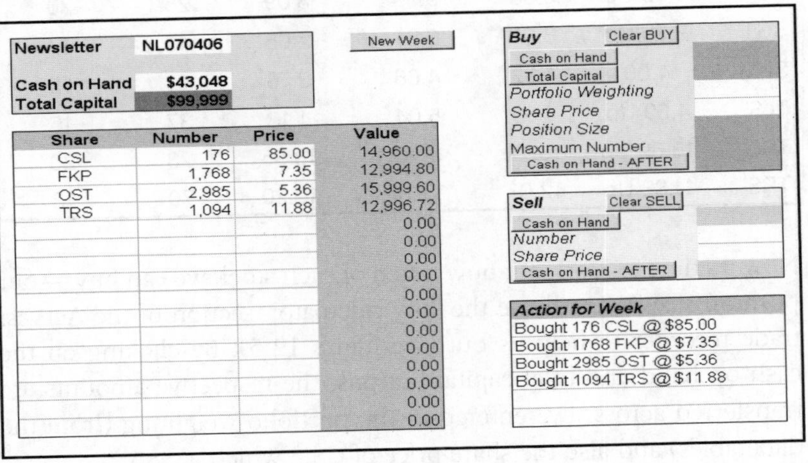

Our total capital now equals the value of our shares plus the cash on hand. Don't worry, we haven't lost a dollar, it's only due to rounding with some of the calculations! Week one is officially over. Now we can sit back and wait for the end of the following week—and then do the same thing all over again.

Week two

It's the end of the week and so now we are ready to go through our steps once again. The first thing to do, which we didn't do in week one, is to check our current positions to see if any of them have been stopped out.

To check our stocks, we look at the data tables and make sure that:

- the stock is still in the data tables, which means it has passed the weekly rate of return criterion
- the weekly closing price is equal to or above the lower deviation.

So far so good—all our stocks are there and all of them are above the lower deviation. Stop losses checked!

Now we can proceed as we did for week one. Once we've checked that both the crossover charts are *not* crossed to the downside, it's time to look at the MMA charts.

Unfortunately, after looking at this week's MMA charts, I've decided that there are none that meet our requirements this week. Some of the charts are promising, but we can leave them for another week. Because we are not doing any buying this week, we don't need to record anything. So that's it for another week.

Week three

It's now week three and, as usual, we are going to check our stop losses using the data tables. We can see that *all* our stocks are still there, meaning they have passed the weekly rate of return, and they are all above their respective lower deviations. A quick look at the newsletter (for the crossover charts) and we can see that we still have the green light, so it's now time to check the MMA charts.

For the sake of this exercise, we'll select ASX for this week and just wait and see on the others. In real time, it will often take up to three months to complete your portfolio, particularly in dull times. But there's no hurry, and patience is definitely your friend.

If we refer to the data tables shown in table 12.2 (overleaf), we can see that the closing price for ASX is in the buy zone and the share price had an up week.

Table 12.2: partial data tables for week three

Share code	Closing price ($)	Central cord ($)	Upper deviation ($)	Lower deviation ($)	ROAR (%)	Port. weighting for 2% risk
ABC	3.78 Up	3.91	4.32	3.26	73	11
AHD	6.71 Dn	7.12	7.67	6.27	41	16
AIX	2.95 Up	2.98	3.22	2.61	36	15
ALL	16.23 Up	17.78	19.14	15.59	20	16
ALZ	2.28 Up	2.31	2.47	2.06	35	18
AMP	10.84 Up	10.91	11.53	10.03	25	20
APZ	2.33 Up	2.58	2.87	2.15	83	11
AQP	39.14 Dn	43.80	49.17	35.10	89	10
ASX	47.81 Up	48.20	52.22	41.69	51	14

To work out our position size, we will refer back to the trade recorder (see figure 12.7), and update the share prices so we can see the current value of our total capital.

Figure 12.7: trade recorder for week three

Newsletter	NL070420		New Week
Cash on Hand	$43,048		
Total Capital	$101,736		

Share	Number	Price	Value
CSL	176	85.00	14,960.00
FKP	1,768	7.31	12,924.08
OST	2,985	5.61	16,745.85
TRS	1,094	12.85	14,057.90
			0.00

Next, we'll update the newsletter field and enter the current share prices from the data tables. We can see that our portfolio has slightly increased in value over the last couple of weeks. The buy calculations for ASX, shown in figure 12.8, will be based on our current total capital. In real time, you would place an order with your broker for $14 243 worth of ASX shares. The broker would then take care of the entry for you and let you know the final price. Please note that you would also need to make them aware of your maximum entry price—the value of the central cord.

Figure 12.8: buy calculator for ASX in week three

Buy	Clear BUY	
Cash on Hand		43,048
Total Capital		101,736
Portfolio Weighting		14
Share Price		47.81
Position Size		14,243
Maximum Number		297
Cash on Hand - AFTER		28,848

Figure 12.9 shows what the trade recorder should look like after updating it with this new purchase.

Figure 12.9: trade recorder at the end of week three

Newsletter	NL070420			New Week		Buy	Clear BUY	
						Cash on Hand		
Cash on Hand	$28,848					Total Capital		
Total Capital	$101,735					Portfolio Weighting		
						Share Price		
Share	Number	Price	Value			Position Size		
CSL	176	85.00	14,960.00			Maximum Number		
FKP	1,768	7.31	12,924.08			Cash on Hand - AFTER		
OST	2,985	5.61	16,745.85					
TRS	1,094	12.85	14,057.90			Sell	Clear SELL	
ASX	297	47.81	14,199.57			Cash on Hand		
			0.00			Number		
			0.00			Share Price		
			0.00			Cash on Hand - AFTER		
			0.00					
			0.00			Action for Week		
			0.00			Bought 297 ASX @ $47.81		
			0.00					
			0.00					
			0.00					
			0.00					
			0.00					

And that's the end of our third week. We still have enough cash for one, maybe two more stocks, but we'll have to wait and see if there are any suitable opportunities. It is perfectly acceptable to leave the money in the bank for the time being, and much more sensible to wait patiently for stocks that meet our requirements.

Week four

The first thing to do of course is to check our stop losses, and by looking at the data tables we can see that they all passed the weekly rate of return search, and they have all closed above their respective lower deviations. We've checked the crossover charts and we've got the green light again, so we'll examine the MMA charts and see if there's anything that looks as if it would fit our portfolio.

After looking at the charts several times and increasing the magnification to see if we can convince ourselves there's something worth buying, we finally decide on Cabcharge (see figure 12.10). It's *very* easy to be a bit cavalier with your selection—although that changes when you realise it's your money on the line. Again, for the sake of this exercise we'll add Cabcharge Australia (CAB) to our portfolio.

Figure 12.10: Cabcharge MMA chart

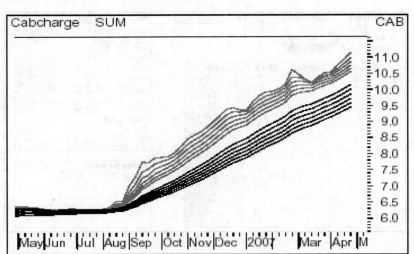

Before working out our position size and so on, we have to check the data tables (see table 12.3) to see if we have a valid entry.

Table 12.3: partial data tables for week four

Share code	Closing price ($)	Central cord ($)	Upper deviation ($)	Lower deviation ($)	ROAR (%)	Port. weighting for 2% risk
ABC	3.51 Dn	3.90	4.32	3.26	73	12
AHD	6.70 Dn	7.15	7.71	6.27	49	16
AIX	2.97 Up	3.01	3.24	2.63	35	15
ALZ	2.30 Up	2.33	2.49	2.06	34	17
AMP	10.86 Up	10.97	11.59	10.03	25	20
APZ	2.34 Up	2.85	2.87	2.15	81	12
AQP	38.36 Dn	43.60	48.93	35.10	85	10
ASX	47.50 Dn	48.85	52.89	42.32	54	14
AWC	7.19 Dn	7.65	8.33	6.55	43	13
AXA	7.54 Dn	7.74	8.33	6.94	27	19
BEN	15.82 Dn	17.93	19.40	15.85	33	17
BLD	8.61 Dn	8.83	9.62	7.56	30	13
BSL	11.69 Up	12.09	13.16	10.35	71	13
CAB	11.32 Up	11.68	12.75	9.94	43	13

Now that we have confirmed that CAB is in the buy zone and has a rate of return greater than 30 per cent, we can update our trade recorder and use the buy calculator to work out the actual position size (see figure 12.11).

Figure 12.11: trade recorder at the end of week four

Newsletter	NL070427			New Week		Buy	Clear BUY	
						Cash on Hand		28,848
Cash on Hand	$15,580					Total Capital		102,130
Total Capital	$102,129					Portfolio Weighting		13
						Share Price		11.32
Share	Number	Price	Value			Position Size		13,277
ASX	297	47.50	14,107.50			Maximum Number		1,172
CSL	176	87.14	15,336.64			Cash on Hand - AFTER		15,580
FKP	1,768	7.04	12,446.72					
OST	2,985	5.77	17,223.45			Sell	Clear SELL	
TRS	1,094	12.95	14,167.30			Cash on Hand		
CAB	1,172	11.32	13,267.04			Number		
			0.00			Share Price		
			0.00			Cash on Hand - AFTER		
			0.00					
			0.00			Action for Week		
			0.00			Bought 1172 CAB @ $11.32		
			0.00					

So that's the end of another week. Six shares in our portfolio and some cash on hand left over to perhaps buy another position.

You've now seen what it takes to be an active investor for a month and it's so simple even our monkey could do it! The time taken each week to go through this process should be less than one hour. In fact, as your skills at MMA chart interpretation develop, you'll find it may take even less time. Once your portfolio is set up, then it's just a matter of checking your stop losses at the end of each week. Please note that you do need to keep checking your stop losses *each* week, as this is a critical part of the risk management process.

Furthermore, the ATO and ASIC will recognise this as a systematic approach to trading shares. This is very important to trustees of self-managed superannuation funds who must be able to provide a written trading plan for their fund on request, and also for those who want to be classified as share traders for tax purposes.

The ActVest newsletter has now been running for over eight years, and is one of the longest running newsletters of its kind in Australia. There's a subscription form for the newsletter at the back of this book. Use this form to receive a free copy of the ActVest trade recorder when you subscribe.

Chapter 13

The downside – short selling using CFDs

Need is the true mother of invention

An inevitable consequence of being exposed to equity markets for a prolonged period of time is exposure to stock market crashes. Because of their magnitude and infrequent occurrence, stock market crashes are perceived to be isolated events, brought about by macro economic circumstances that are a function of a unique or highly infrequent moment in the global business cycle.

Once the economists have performed their post mortem on a crash, a wave of economic reforms is implemented. Regulatory bodies are given greater powers to ensure that the speculators and corporate cowboys behave themselves in future. Powerful political, economic and industrial figures have private meetings, supposedly to orchestrate their efforts at ensuring the long-term prosperity of humankind, from which they each emerge stating that everything is going to be okay.

The man in the street forgets all about becoming rich in the stock market and returns to his job; content in the knowledge he has a roof over his head, a shirt on his back and food on the table. After a narrow escape with financial Armageddon we collectively adopt the attitude, world leaders and general public alike, that fiscal exuberance is the root of all evil, and begin the monotonous task of consolidating our debt. Governments balance their budgets and we pay off our credit cards. As long as the painful memory of the aftermath of a crash lingers there will be little chance of a capitalist orgy that precedes a crash ever occurring again.

As we look back over the centuries, the crashes of the past act as punctuation marks in global economic history. They pinpoint the hard economic lessons that have been committed to memory in the form of university textbooks. Here, they serve as high doctrine to future world leaders and the other apprentice keepers of the global economy.

The working classes who suffered in the aftermath but did not participate in the orgy of instant wealth will remember the event, and those who participated in it, with complete disdain. They will tell their children and their children's children of the corporate greed that brought about unemployment and thinner pay packets. In doing so, they will perpetuate the desire among the working class to insulate themselves from the folly of capitalism with instruments of solidarity, such as workers' unions. And so another crash will be committed to history.

But here's the kicker. While the human race evolves both economically and industrially, human psychology remains constant. History repeats itself because we repeat previous actions that are a function of our psychological makeup. Every time there is a repetition in stock market speculation we trot out the well-worn line, 'But things are different this time'.

In the technology boom of the 1990s, the basis for differentiating current circumstances from previous speculative orgies was the advent of the internet and other technological marvels. Table 13.1 compares this recent technological revolution with that of the early 1900s.

Table 13.1: technological developments of the 20th century

Early 1900s	Late 1900s
Motor car	Internet
Flight	Satellites
Radio	Mobile phones
Telephone	Space travel
Moving pictures	Computers

While the underlying reason for each boom is always different, in essence they are all the same. Technology and industry will always evolve. Human psychology, our needs and desires, on the other hand, remain constant. Circumstances are similar but never the same. And stock market crashes are inevitable. But it isn't the occurrence of a stock market crash itself that I fear—I know from experience that it's the aftermath that does the damage. Consider figure 13.1, which shows the Dow Jones Industrial Average around the time of the great stock market crash of 1929.

Figure 13.1: Dow Jones Industrial Average chart showing the 1929 crash

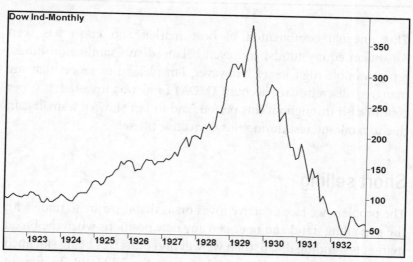

Investors can lose a lot of money in stock market crashes but a sustained bear market, such as the one that followed the 1929 crash, can completely wipe you out. In a more recent example, the following chart of the All Ordinaries Index (figure 13.2) shows the massive slide the Australian stock market suffered during the 2007–08 market correction. This is by far the largest fall we've seen since the 1987 stock market crash, which saw the All Ordinaries drop nearly 50 per cent from 2300 to just 1200 points.

Figure 13.2: All Ordinaries chart for 2007–08

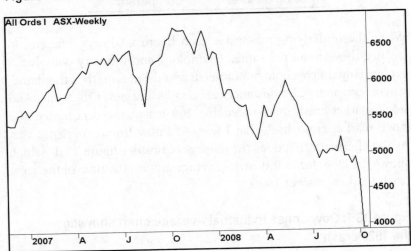

This unusual combination of bear market and crash has seen Australian equity funds, and even balanced superannuation funds, report double digit losses. However, I'm pleased to report that my managed discretionary account (MDA) fund was invested 100 per cent in cash throughout this period, and in fact showed a small gain due to bank interest during this corrective phase.

Short selling

The problem we face as active investors is that if we are to trade with the prevailing trend and not open any new positions when the broad market is trending down, then we will find ourselves being sidelined during periods such as that which occurred in 2007–08. To prevent this from happening, as it did with my MDA fund, we need to have the ability to profit in bear market conditions.

To do this we need to 'short sell' ordinary shares, that is, to sell shares we don't own with the intention of buying them back later, at a cheaper price. The best way to explain short selling is to use an analogy. The following example illustrates how we can profit from selling an item before we buy it:

- imagine you rent a new TV from Acme Rentals
- the rent is $100 per annum
- you *sell* the TV to Fred Nurk for $600
- one year later you buy the TV back for $400, making a profit of $200
- you then return the TV to Acme Rentals and pay the $100 rent
- therefore, your net profit after the rent of $100 is paid is $100.

Unfortunately, it is illegal to sell goods that you don't have clear title to and so we can't profit from short selling tangible goods that we can rent. However, there are many ways in which we can actually short sell ordinary shares, with the easiest and most convenient way being contracts for difference, or CFDs. CFDs make short selling ordinary shares extremely easy. I don't want to go into too much depth about the mechanics of short selling with CFDs, but I can assure you that any CFD broker would gladly assist you with such an enquiry. I personally use Braden Gardiner at Sonray Capital Markets and he can be contacted at <b.gardiner@sonray.com.au>.

... when you short sell using CFDs you actually get paid interest.

Put simply, when you place a trade into a CFD account you nominate whether you want to trade long or short. This means that you can nominate to either buy shares (the conventional way of trading) or sell shares (short selling). In the former instance you will profit in a rising market and in the latter case from a falling market.

But there's also a nice little bonus. If you trade long with CFDs you have to pay interest, whereas when you short sell using CFDs you are actually *paid* interest. Note that you are responsible for the payment of any distributions by the underlying shares you short sell, and you must therefore weigh up the cost of paying dividends against the interest you'll receive. This means that some care must be taken not to short sell companies that pay high dividend yields, but from personal experience I can confidently say that this is not an overly prohibitive issue.

And here's some more good news—when trading a rising share, as the share price rises, the rate of return diminishes. This means that as the trend gets older it becomes less and less profitable, but this situation is reversed when short selling. While there is obviously a downside limit as to how far we can short sell the price of a share ($0.00), the closer you get to $0.00, the more profitable the trade becomes in proportional terms.

However, there is for some of us a psychological discomfort in obtaining financial gain from someone else's demise. If you fall into this category or find the science of short selling difficult to comprehend—don't do it. It is not an essential component of the active investing strategy, and the stock market is not a place where anyone should be operating outside their comfort zone.

Dynamic analysis

On the basis that we are comfortable with the idea of short selling then all we have to do is turn our existing strategy upside down. Figure 13.3 depicts the inverted market dynamic for short selling.

Figure 13.3: dynamic analysis for short selling

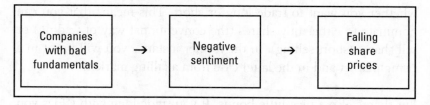

Unfortunately, Wrightbooks doesn't publish a book on stocks with bad fundamentals, poor future prospects or incompetent manag-ement. This means we will have to do the bulk of the research ourselves. However, the StockDoctor program mentioned earlier in the book will locate companies with bad fundamentals, as well as those with good fundamentals. And, as with trading long, a scan of the top 500 companies for those with poor fundamentals will create a pool of about 150 shares for us to subject to further analysis.

Rate of decline indicator

Short selling uses an upside down version of the conventional approach, with the rate of return indicator becoming the 'rate of decline' indicator. The mathematics behind the rate of decline (RoD) indicator is identical to the rate of return indicator except that we are now searching for shares that are *falling* at a rate of at least 20 per cent per annum (for the MetaStock formula for the RoD indicator see appendix A).

The chart of company M (figure 13.4) demonstrates the use of the RoD indicator, which can be seen with a horizontal cut-off bar set at 20 per cent. This example also illustrates how the rate of decline actually increases as the price of the share approaches zero. This is a particularly useful characteristic if you wish to increase the size of your position as it moves further into profit, as the profitability of the trade will increase along with your position size.

Figure 13.4: company M share price chart showing RoD indicator

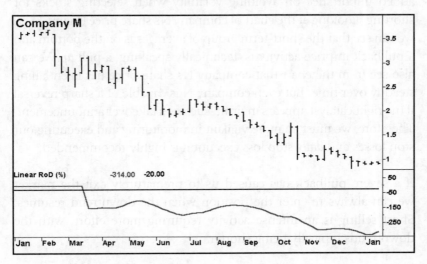

Upside down MMA charts

While reversing the active investing strategy so far has been relatively straightforward, the sentiment that drives equity markets up is not the exact reverse of the sentiment that pushes share prices down. Bulls run on greed, while bears are driven by fear, and these emotional forces are unfortunately not mirror images of each other.

Therefore, given this lack of symmetry, we need to use a slightly modified set of tactics for trading the market on the short side. The most noticeable difference is that the bears act with greater impetus but in shorter bursts than the bulls. Historical examination of stock markets supports this observation, as global markets will rise for much longer periods than they fall but will fall with greater speed.

Furthermore, the majority of human beings are optimists and react swiftly when a glimmer of hope appears on the horizon. Therefore, short-term factors that affect opinion have a greater influence than when trading long because they will work in harmony with people's optimism to rapidly lift share prices.

When searching through the MMA charts we will discover that volatility is harder to avoid and that the regular pullbacks in the short-term group of averages is more pronounced. We must place added importance on avoiding volatility when selecting stocks for shorting. Looking at the chart of company N's share price (figure 13.5) we can see that the short-term group of averages is on the bottom and a pullback in price activity is, technically speaking, a pull *up*. We can also see from the chart that company N's share price has been falling steadily over time. But even company N is capable of a sharp reversal if the right catalyst appears in print, such as a takeover announcement. Therefore, we must be more vigilant in monitoring and executing our stop losses and *daily* stop loss execution is highly recommended.

If a severe pullback has caused us to prematurely exit the market we can always re-enter the position when the downtrend resumes. Short selling is an intense activity requiring more effort, with the downtrends typically being shorter.

Figure 13.5: company N share price chart

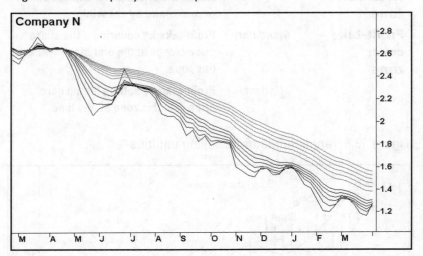

The range indicator in reverse

Thankfully, where the range indicator is concerned, it is a case of simply doing everything the opposite way. Applying the range indicator to short selling means transposing all of our rules from buying and selling to shorting and covering, where covering is the act of buying back the shares we originally short sold.

Figure 13.6 (overleaf) shows the range indicator for falling equities, where the upper deviation is displaced by two and a half times the 13-week average true range, and the lower deviation is displaced by three times. In the case of short selling, the upper deviation is prevented from rising instead of the lower deviation being prevented from falling. The rules I use for the short selling zones are:

Stop loss — cover zone	**Cover** if the share price closes at the end of the day in this zone.
Short/hold zone	**Short sell** if the share price has closed at the end of the week in this zone lower than the previous week. The price must be between the upper deviation and the central cord.
	Hold if already owned.

Hold/cover zone		**Hold** if the share price is in this zone or **profit-take by covering**.
Profit-take — cover zone	*Mandatory*	**Profit-take by covering** if the share price closes at the end of the week in this zone.
	Optional	**Profit-take by selling** if the share price is in this zone at any time.

Figure 13.6: range indicator for falling equities

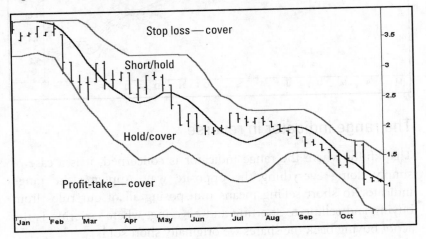

Don't tell anyone

On a final note, it's worth mentioning that if you do trade short while the market is falling and most people are losing money, then it's probably best to keep your good fortune to yourself. After the great crash of 1929, there was a US congressional enquiry into short selling, as many investors felt that this practice was the root cause of the stock market's collapse.

There is no doubt however, that our perspective will shift dramatically now that we have the ability to turn what was previously adversity into advantage. Figure 13.7 shows some of the short selling opportunities that presented themselves during the correction of 2007–08. Further information on short selling using the active investing strategy is supplied in the ActVest newsletter (see page 212).

Figure 13.7: short selling opportunities in 2007–08

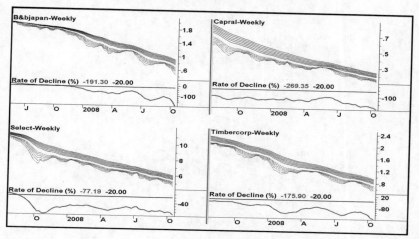

Chapter 14
The big picture

The trick is being able to see both the wood and the trees

The football analogy at the end of chapter one looked at the difference between being on the oval in the thick of the action, as opposed to sitting at the top of the grandstand and taking in the whole picture. In the last few chapters we have looked, in detail, at the techniques we need to employ at ground level. Although we make no pretence at being omnipresent in the marketplace, our strategy encompasses all the following areas and more:

- fundamental analysis
- technical analysis (charting)
- broad market analysis
- cyclical analysis
- sector analysis
- macro economics

- risk management
- short selling.

In this final chapter we will sit up in the grandstand once again, and look at some of the more pertinent big picture issues we need to address as active investors.

House cleaning

The very first obstacle we encounter when taking the plunge into active investing for the first time, is having to do our initial house cleaning. House cleaning refers to the process of evaluating and cleaning up the existing portfolio of shares we have accumulated prior to implementing the active investing strategy.

Some of the shares we already own will fall into the category of 'stock-in-trade' shares and some will fall into the category of 'asset class' shares—definitions we discussed earlier in chapter three. As active investors we can continue to hold any shares that fall into either of these two categories.

The hard part of this process is biting the bullet and selling any shares that don't belong in either category. This can be a bit like parting with our favourite pair of old runners. Added to this heartache is the confusion of not knowing how to tackle what can be a lengthy and confusing process, depending on the size of your existing holdings.

As with most potentially daunting tasks, it pays to tackle the job of house cleaning with a step-by-step approach in order of priority. And while I can't do your house cleaning for you, I can offer you a step-by-step procedure to follow.

Step one: capital allocation

We start by drawing a financial road map for our whole shares strategy. The key question being; what proportion of our entire capital do we want to allocate to stock-in-trade shares, and what proportion to asset class shares? As our answer won't be set in stone, don't panic if you're unsure on this question.

If you're young, then you'll probably want to actively manage your portfolio and you will want very little exposure to asset class shares, or possibly no exposure at all. On the other hand, you may be considerably older and not having to actively manage all of your shares will be very desirable. If you fall into this latter category, then you may also already have some very high-yielding stocks that you would be loathe to part with. Either way, this is a question you can come back to later if you change your mind.

Step two: stock-in-trade shares

As active investing is primarily a share trading strategy, it should be safe to assume that this is our primary interest in the stock market and therefore, it would be sensible to start by identifying any stock-in-trade shares we already own. This is a relatively straightforward task because, according to our active investing criteria, we want to retain any fundamentally sound blue-chip shares that are rising in price. These shares will be managed from now on using the strategy outlined in this book.

Step three: asset class shares

Once we've identified any stock-in-trade shares and put them to one side, it's time to move on to any potential asset class shares we already own, or wish to buy. However, as you will shortly see, assessing shares as lifetime income-producing assets is not a simple process—just ask Warren Buffett. In seeking lifetime income-producing assets, we must consider the following three areas:

- lifetime—asset class shares represent companies that will exist for our lifetime
- income—asset class shares must have an acceptable dividend yield
- assets—asset class shares should represent companies with sound fundamentals.

But before delving further into each of these areas, it is important to mention that each of us has a different set of financial circumstances and goals, and we are all of different ages. Therefore, the guidelines offered here are not set in stone and should be tailored to each individual's current lifestyle and needs.

Lifetime

In order to make a judgement as to whether a publicly listed company will last our lifetime, we must first quantify our own life expectancy and then determine the life expectancy of the company in question. As human life expectancy is well beyond the scope of this discussion we will quickly move on to the question of company life expectancy.

There are several guidelines we can combine in order to estimate a company's life expectancy. The main problem is that we are required to make qualitative judgments about the stability of different commercial operating environments, that is, we have to make an assessment of the longevity and stability of different industry sectors.

In this regard, Warren Buffett's choices are epitomised by the companies he has acquired in the past. He believes that men will always have to shave so he has bought shares in Gillette, whereas he completely abstained from the 'tech' boom on the simple basis that he perceived the operating environment to be subject to rapid change—a sensible assessment.

Another guideline we can employ is to look at the size of a company in terms of its market capitalisation. The simple logic here is that the bigger a company is, the less likely it is to disappear off the face of the earth. Mind you, owners of HIH shares and Enron in the United States might disagree with this logic.

But while size doesn't necessarily ensure survival, it is a statistically valid approach, with the vast majority of delistings occurring among companies with smaller capitalisation. For asset class shares I recommend a cut-off of $100 million as a minimum, as this level fairly accurately defines the top 500 stocks listed on the ASX.

Of course we still need to assess each company on its own merits, as there are always individual circumstances that can't be incorporated into global benchmarks. A typical example of this would be ANZ or Westpac. These banks would become likely takeover targets for the larger banks in the event of the dismantling of the 'four pillar' banking policy by the federal government. Therefore, the four pillar policy could have a direct effect on the life expectancy of these companies at some point in the future. We need to apply our best judgement in this area and also fully accept that circumstances beyond our control can and will alter the life expectancy of public companies over time. As you can now see, this is not an exact science.

Income

As the average dividend yield of the entire stock market has a very strong tendency to track official interest rates, our expectations in terms of income must remain flexible and in keeping with the Reserve Bank of Australia's official cash interest rate. As the average dividend yield is usually just *below* the official cash interest rate, it would be prudent to set our minimum benchmark just *above* the Reserve Bank's official rate. This will ensure that our income stream is always greater than the official cash rate and therefore, that we're always ahead of the curve. What's more, this benchmark doesn't take into consideration any franking credits, for example, tax credits, to which we may also be entitled.

... guidelines should be tailored to [your] current lifestyle and needs.

It is also important to ensure that when calculating the yield you apply the current annual dividend payment to your original purchase price, and not to the current price of the share if you bought them previously. For example, if you paid $6.50 for CBA shares in 1991, then the annual dividend of approximately $2.70 per share (at the time of writing) represents an annual income stream of about 40 per cent.On the other hand, it equates to a dividend yield of only 6.5per cent with respect to the current share price.

Finally, it is always wise to make sure that the 'dividend per share', or DPS, is not of an abnormal nature and is in keeping with the normal dividend payment pattern of the company. In other words, check that the company has not paid out an extraordinarily large dividend because its income has been abnormally inflated due to a unique circumstance, such as the selling of a major asset. An example of this was when Mayne Nickless sold its interest in Optus many years ago, which led to a bonus payment to shareholders of an extra $1 per share.

Assets

This area is fairly straightforward. If you are to retain your asset class shares for a lifetime then obviously the company they represent must have sound fundamentals. Once again, I use *Top Stocks* by Martin Roth and StockDoctor by Lincoln Indictors to evaluate the fundamentals of publicly listed companies.

The very broad guidelines given here should help you in deciding whether or not shares already in your possession qualify as asset class shares. Furthermore, the same set of guidelines applies equally if you are considering acquiring new shares as lifetime income-producing assets. But, and I'm sure Buffet would agree, these guidelines are of a very general nature only and I would strongly recommend further study in this area if it is of specific interest to you. A list of potential asset class stocks is also provided in the ActVest newsletter each week.

Step four: sell the rest

Any shares that are left over after completing steps one to three should be sold—quickly, like tearing off a bandaid. It's good practice. The toughest thing you'll ever do in the stock market is sell.

Step five: position sizing

Now that we've decided on which shares are staying and which ones are going, we have to make sure we're not overweight in any individual position or sector. For this step, you need to treat stock-in-trade shares and asset class shares as being mutually exclusive. In other words, your total capital in each case is completely separate, and you should consider these two pools of shares as two totally separate portfolios.

> **Question:** Can I own a share as both an asset class share and a stock-in-trade share?

> **Answer:** Yes—simply hold a separate allocation of the same share in each portfolio.

My allocation of total capital per sector, in the case of either stock-in-trade trade or asset class shares, is 30 per cent. My maximum position size for asset class shares alone is 10 per cent of total capital, while it's 20 per cent for stock-in-trade shares.

We can be more aggressive in the case of stock-in-trade shares because we are managing these investments with the aid of a stop loss, which will limit any downside risk. On the other hand, if we are unlucky enough to buy into a company like HIH as an asset class share, then the only safeguard that will mitigate our losses would be if we limit our capital allocation to a reasonably conservative amount, such as 10 per cent or less.

Hope and tax

Whenever I discuss house cleaning with newcomers to the stock market, two objections are always raised—hope and tax. Hope is where a stock's share price has crashed down to the point that selling it would barely cover brokerage, so you think why not just hang on to it in the hope that it will recover one day. In this instance I recommend selling the shares because you probably need the practice.

Retaining a bad investment for tax purposes is no way to run a sound business. Ask any shopkeeper what they do with their dead stock and they'll reply, 'Mark it down and sell it'. I know this advice sounds tough, but the hardest thing for any investor to do is to let go of a bad investment and move on. On a positive note, investors who are prepared to do so will generally sleep better as a result.

Taking an income

Of course there is another reason I need to sell my shares — income. As an active investor, my objective is to make at least 20 per cent per annum on a consistent basis. This is all well and good but as any share trader will attest, you can't eat a portfolio — even if it is growing at 20 per cent per annum.

Paper profits are exactly that until you sell down your portfolio, converting them into cash. So, apart from the privileged few who don't rely on their share portfolio for their ongoing living expenses, trimming the portfolio to convert it to an income is a common reality.

Now we have the question of how to trim a share portfolio without hurting it. In response, a valid analogy would be the type of trimming that gardeners do, given that a well-trimmed portfolio is healthy and will continue to grow well, whereas poor trimming can cause the type of harm only time will heal. The best way to demonstrate how to trim a portfolio is to use a hypothetical example. Let's start with a portfolio of eight stocks and their initial values, shown in table 14.1.

Table 14.1: example share portfolio

Stock	Value
DEF	$50 000
GHI	$50 000
JKL	$50 000
MNO	$50 000
PQR	$50 000
TUV	$50 000
WXY	$50 000
ZZZ	$50 000
Total capital	**$400 000**

The first rule is not to nibble at your portfolio as your living expenses dictate. This approach will make your stockbroker very happy as you'll be helping with their living expenses, but it will be a costly and cumbersome approach for you. You need to establish a *separate* cash reserve that you will live out of and that can be periodically 'topped up' using your portfolio.

So, as part of our initial set-up we will also include a separate bank account containing $50 000 which will keep us in the very comfortable lifestyle to which we are accustomed for a period of *at least six months*. Now, let's assume we are six months on. Our situation is shown in table 14.2.

Table 14.2: share portfolio six months on

Stock	Value
DEF	$95 000
GHI	$45 000
JKL	$55 000
MNO	$55 000
PQR	$60 000
TUV	$53 000
WXY	$47 000
Cash	$40 000
Total capital	**$450 000**
Cash for living expenses	**$10 000**

We've sold ZZZ converting it into $40 000 cash, which is part of our portfolio and still included in our calculation for total capital but kept separate from our cash for living expenses. So we now have seven open positions, plus some cash on hand. As we need to replace $40 000 cash for our living expenses ($50 000 starting balance less current balance of $10 000), it seems obvious that we would just transfer the cash from our portfolio. This would be easy, but wrong.

Firstly, we must calculate what the total capital will be once we take out the $40 000 we need. Next, we check all our positions to see if we are overweight in any, that is, greater than 20 per cent in any individual position. Trim any such positions back to 20 per cent of \$410 000 and then dip into the cash on hand if we still need more. Our results can be seen in table 14.3.

Table 14.3: share portfolio after trimming

Stock	Value
DEF	\$82 000
GHI	\$45 000
JKL	\$55 000
MNO	\$55 000
PQR	\$60 000
TUV	\$53 000
WXY	\$47 000
Cash	\$13 000
Total capital	**\$410 000**
Cash for living expenses	**\$50 000**

As it turns out, the only position to be trimmed is DEF by \$13 000 and the remaining \$27 000 comes from the cash on hand. While it would appear that we've just kicked the goose that lays the golden egg by selling down DEF our best performing stock, in fact we have just put it back in its place. We can't afford to let any individual goose rule the roost. Although we don't want to cull the winners from our portfolio, we don't want it to become lopsided either. Of course, a more common scenario is when there is no cash on hand to dip into, as shown in table 14.4.

Table 14.4: share portfolio without cash on hand

Stock	Value
DEF	\$95 000
GHI	\$45 000
JKL	\$55 000
MNO	\$55 000
PQR	\$60 000
TUV	\$53 000
WXY	\$47 000

Stock	Value
ZZZ	$40 000
Total capital	**$450 000**
Cash for living expenses	**$10 000**

In this situation, where there is no cash on hand to make up the difference, the only option is to trim across the entire portfolio, after we have trimmed back any overweight positions such as DEF. The calculations to work out how much to trim from each position are as follows:

- after trimming DEF by $13 000 (back to $82 000) we still need another $27 000

- divide the amount required by the number of stocks, including DEF ($27 000 ÷ 8 = $3375)

- therefore, the amount to trim from each position would be $3375.

Putting the process in order of priority—trim any overweight positions, then dip into cash on hand and lastly, if necessary trim all open positions evenly, and without fear or favour.

Constant vigilance

Now, here's the bad news. The reason why so many ready-made trading systems don't work is because they assume that all factors, for example, people and financial markets, remain constant. However, the only constant that we should concern ourselves with is the need for constant vigilance in reviewing our strategy. What works for us today will not necessarily work for us tomorrow. We must revisit our strategy and its benchmarks on a regular basis to ensure they are still valid. For instance, if world markets become nervous and volatile then it may be prudent to use daily stop losses instead of weekly stop losses—a sensible change in policy during times such as those experienced in 2007–08.

In any evolving business environment, an out-of-date rule book will inevitably become self-defeating. What's more, our personal goals and business objectives will change with the passage of time so we need to review and update these on a regular basis. Personally, I like to review the performance of my investment strategy and objectives at least once a year.

Test and measure

If these reviews are to be productive, not to mention easy, we must have accurate data at our disposal. We can't implement change if we don't know what it is that we're changing. Business consultants will often lament the fact that the majority of small business owners don't know what they're doing wrong because they don't know what they're doing, let alone what they're doing right. So the first step for most small business makeovers (this includes investors), is the implementation of proper testing and measuring procedures.

When people talk to me about their stock market strategy it is usually a short conversation. This is because I ask embarrassing questions such as, 'Do you use daily or weekly stops?' or, 'What was your portfolio's annual rate of return last year?' These questions are embarrassing for a lot of people because they don't test and measure what they're doing, or because they constantly tweak their investment strategy as they go along.

You won't know if something works unless you implement it for a reasonable period of time and test and measure the results. I know what does and doesn't work because I test and measure everything I do. This includes my mistakes, of which I make plenty but rarely repeat.

Organisation

When I was in high school in the 1970s, a study was conducted to identify common behavioural traits among highly successful students. The only common factor found was organisational ability. Successful students knew their strengths and weaknesses, allocated their time, and kept impeccably organised class notes.

Success in business is also dependent on organisational ability, as there is little point in testing and measuring our market performance if we fail to properly record the results. I maintain a hand-written trading ledger where I record every trade I have ever executed. A trading ledger is essential and it should include, at minimum, the following fields:

- *date*—the date the transaction was completed
- *buy or sell*—the type of transaction (buying or selling)
- *stock/code*—the name of the stock and ASX code
- *quantity*—the number of shares being bought or sold
- *price*—the price per share of the transaction
- *profit*—the net profit, including brokerage, GST, etc. (completed trades only)
- *loss*—the net loss (completed trades only)
- *cumulative profit and loss*—a running sum total of the profit and loss columns.

I fill out my trading ledger when I receive the buy and sell contracts. This prompts me to fill out the ledger, and the figures given in the contracts include costs such as brokerage, and so on. So whenever I review my trading rules I have solid evidence on which to base my decisions. If I am happy with my performance then I can confidently carry all my existing trading tactics and benchmarks forward. If my performance is below par then I can usually determine the problem and alter my strategy accordingly.

Acquire knowledge as your need dictates

As anyone who has ever started a small business will attest, you will encounter many problems on the road ahead—big and small, technical and psychological. Save your brain capacity for dealing with these unexpected potholes. When I had been trading for one year I had one year's market experience, and after five years of trading I had five years' experience. There is no short cut through this process, so don't try to replace market experience with market knowledge.

Acquire knowledge out of need and not out of desire. There is no question that the market will always be there tomorrow and this book provides enough knowledge to ensure that you will be too.

Appendix A
MetaStock indicator formulas

The following formulas, developed by Simon Sherwood, are designed for use on weekly charts only.

Rate of return and rate of decline indicators

200*(LinearReg(C,52)-Ref(LinearReg(C,52),-26))/C

Exploration — rate of return

Rate of Return > 20

Exploration — rate of decline

Rate of Decline < -20

Range indicator — rising equities

Central cord

LinearReg(C,13);

Lower deviation

If(LinearReg(C,13)>PREV,If(LinearReg(C,13)-(ATR(13)*2.5)>PREV, LinearReg(C,13)-(ATR(13)*2.5),PREV),LinearReg(C,13));

Upper deviation

LinearReg(C,13)+(ATR(13)*3);

Range indicator — falling equities

Central cord

LinearReg(C,13);

Lower deviation

LinearReg(C,13)-(ATR(13)*3);

Upper deviation

If(LinearReg(C,13)<PREV,If(LinearReg(C,13)+(ATR(13)*2.5)<PREV,
LinearReg(C,13)+(ATR(13)*2.5),PREV),LinearReg(C,13));

MMA charts

MetaStock users can either build MMA indicators or create an MMA template.

Short-term group of exponential moving averages — 3, 5, 7, 9, 11 and 13.

Long-term group of exponential moving averages — 21, 24, 27, 30, 33 and 36.

Sector rate of return

200*(LinearReg(C,52)-Ref(LinearReg(C,52),-26))/C

Further reading

Blue Chip Investing, Alan Hull (Wrightbooks)

Charting in a Nutshell, Alan Hull (Wrightbooks)

Top Stocks, Martin Roth (Wiley)

Buffettology, Mary Buffett (Simon & Schuster)

Trading for a Living, Dr Alexander Elder (Wiley)

Rich Dad, Poor Dad, Robert T. Kiyosaki (Techpress Inc.)

One Up on Wall Street, Peter Lynch (Simon & Schuster)

Reminiscences of a Stock Operator, Edwin Lefevre (Wiley)

Index

ActVest newsletter subscription form

The ActVest newsletter is updated every week and as a subscriber...

- you don't need to buy and understand complicated computer programs
- you won't have to pay for ongoing and expensive data feeds
- you will spend less than one hour a week managing your portfolio
- you can cancel your subscription at any time.

Please print all details clearly, tick where appropriate, sign, date and fax or post to:

ActVest P/L
53 Grange Drive
Lysterfield
Victoria, 3156

Fax 03 9778 7062

YES ☐   I wish to subscribe to the ActVest newsletter at $39.50 per month, plus the joining fee of $49.50 AND receive as a bonus the ActVest trade recorder FREE (valued at $49.50)

Please charge my credit card:

Visa ☐   Mastercard ☐

Card no. __ __ __ __   __ __ __ __   __ __ __ __   __ __ __ __

Expiry date: __ / __

Full name: _____

Email address: _____

Daytime phone: _____

Signature: .... Date: /   /

I acknowledge that ActVest ABN-64 258 679 725 must retain my credit card details for the purpose of charging me $39.50 on the 1st day of each month. Should I elect to discontinue my subscription, I must notify ActVest in writing.

ActVest newsletter contents

The ActVest newsletter contains all the information needed to implement the strategies outlined in this book. Each newsletter includes:

- long-term MMA charts of the US S&P 500 index and the All Ordinaries index

- short-term crossover charts for the US S&P 500 index and the All Ordinaries index

- sector analysis charts for all 24 S&P GICS industry sectors, including RoR and MMAs

- data tables for blue-chip stocks that are rising or falling in price at more than 20 per cent per annum. These tables include closing price (including price direction), range indicator values, rate of return values and the portfolio weighting for the two per cent risk rule

- MMA charts for all equities listed in the data tables. These charts can be amplified for closer examination using the zoom function in Adobe Acrobat Reader program which can be downloaded free from the internet.

If you would like to receive a free sample of the ActVest newsletter, please send an email to enquiries@actvest.com. We'll also add you to our email database so we can keep you informed about upcoming seminars and Traders Club meetings in Melbourne, Sydney and Brisbane.

Alan Hull an authorised representative of Gryphon Learning, holder of Australian Financial Services Licence No. 246606 and registered training organisation provider No. 21327. For further details on Gryphon's Australian Financial Services Licence please visit the website www.alanhull.com